ROYAL CHILDREN

Queen Victoria with four great-grandchildren in 1900: Prince Edward of York (standing), Princess Mary and Prince Albert (sitting), and Prince Henry in the Queen's arms.

ROYAL CHILDREN

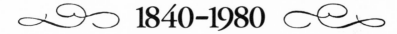 1840-1980

From Queen Victoria to Queen Elizabeth II

Celia Clear

STEIN AND DAY/*Publishers*/New York

For my Mother

First published in the United States of America in 1981
Copyright © 1981 by Celia Clear
Printed in the United States of America
Stein and Day/*Publishers*/Scarborough House
Briarcliff Manor, New York 10510

Library of Congress Cataloging in Publication Data
Clear, Celia.
  Royal children, 1840–1980.

  Bibliography: p.
  Includes index.
  1. Great Britain—Princes and princesses.   I. Title.
DA28.3.C46 1981   941.08'092'2 [B]   81-5289
ISBN 0-8128-2826-7   AACR2

Contents

INTRODUCTION 7

1 Victoria's Nursery 13

2 Sunshine and Shadow 27

3 Darling Motherdear 52

4 Sailor Princes 71

5 The Little Princesses 93

6 Outward Bound 116

BIOGRAPHICAL NOTES 134

SELECT BIBLIOGRAPHY 139

ACKNOWLEDGEMENTS 142

INDEX 143

Four generations: Queen Victoria, Edward VII, George V and the infant Edward VIII.

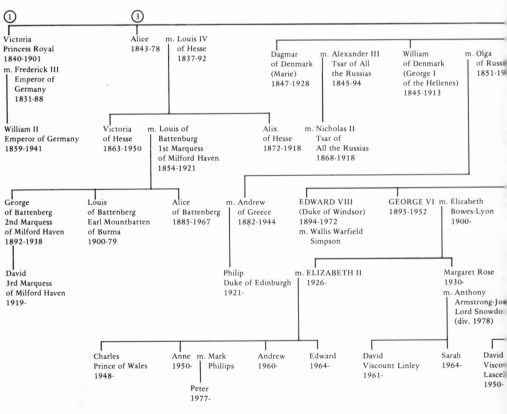

①   ③

Victoria
Princess Royal
1840-1901
m. Frederick III
Emperor of
Germany
1831-88

Alice   m. Louis IV
1843-78   of Hesse
         1837-92

Dagmar   m. Alexander III
of Denmark   Tsar of All
(Marie)   the Russias
1847-1928   1845-94

William   m. Olga
of Denmark   of Russi
(George I   1851-19
of the Hellenes)
1845-1913

William II
Emperor of Germany
1859-1941

Victoria   m. Louis of
of Hesse   Battenburg
1863-1950   1st Marquess
       of Milford Haven
       1854-1921

Alix   m. Nicholas II
of Hesse   Tsar of
1872-1918   All the Russias
       1868-1918

George
of Battenberg
2nd Marquess
of Milford Haven
1892-1938

Louis
of Battenberg
Earl Mountbatten
of Burma
1900-79

Alice   m. Andrew
of Battenberg   of Greece
1885-1967   1882-1944

EDWARD VIII
(Duke of Windsor)
1894-1972
m. Wallis Warfield
Simpson

GEORGE VI   m. Elizabeth
1895-1952   Bowes-Lyon
           1900-

David
3rd Marquess
of Milford Haven
1919-

Philip   m. ELIZABETH II
Duke of Edinburgh   1926-
1921-

Margaret Rose
1930-
m. Anthony
Armstrong-Jo
Lord Snowdo
(div. 1978)

Charles
Prince of Wales
1948-

Anne   m. Mark
1950- | Phillips

Andrew
1960-

Edward
1964-

David
Viscount Linley
1961-

Sarah
1964-

David
Visco
Lasce
1950-

Peter
1977-

The House of Windsor:
Descendants of Queen Victoria

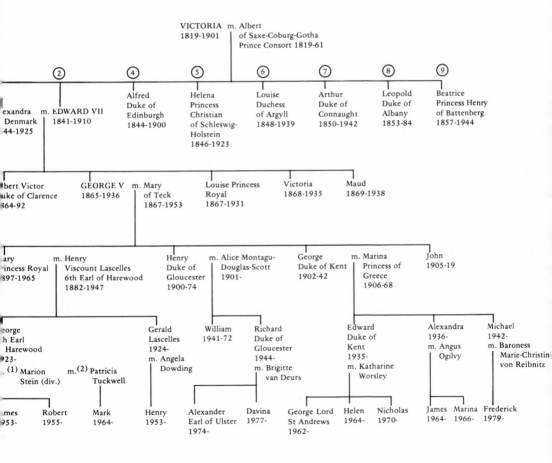

VICTORIA m. Albert
1819-1901 of Saxe-Coburg-Gotha
Prince Consort 1819-61

② ④ ⑤ ⑥ ⑦ ⑧ ⑨

Alfred
Duke of
Edinburgh
1844-1900

Helena
Princess
Christian
of Schleswig-
Holstein
1846-1923

Louise
Duchess
of Argyll
1848-1939

Arthur
Duke of
Connaught
1850-1942

Leopold
Duke of
Albany
1853-84

Beatrice
Princess Henry
of Battenberg
1857-1944

exandra m. EDWARD VII
Denmark 1841-1910
44-1925

bert Victor   GEORGE V m. Mary
uke of Clarence   1865-1936   of Teck
864-92   1867-1953

Louise Princess
Royal
1867-1931

Victoria
1868-1935

Maud
1869-1938

ary   m. Henry
rincess Royal Viscount Lascelles
897-1965   6th Earl of Harewood
              1882-1947

Henry   m. Alice Montagu-
Duke of   Douglas-Scott
Gloucester   1901-
1900-74

George   m. Marina
Duke of Kent   Princess of
1902-42   Greece
               1906-68

John
1905-19

eorge
h Earl
Harewood
23-
(1) Marion   m.(2) Patricia
   Stein (div.)   Tuckwell

Gerald
Lascelles
1924-
m. Angela
Dowding

William
1941-72

Richard
Duke of
Gloucester
1944-
m. Brigitte
van Deurs

Edward
Duke of
Kent
1935-
m. Katharine
Worsley

Alexandra
1936-
m. Angus
Ogilvy

Michael
1942-
m. Baroness
Marie-Christine
von Reibnitz

mes   Robert   Mark
953-   1955-   1964-

Henry
1953-

Alexander   Davina
Earl of Ulster 1977-
1974-

George Lord   Helen   Nicholas
St Andrews   1964-   1970-
1962-

James   Marina   Frederick
1964-   1966-   1979-

Introduction

Upon the good education of Princes, and especially of those
who are destined to govern, the welfare of the world in these
days greatly depends.

Albert, Prince Consort, 1849

*A*LL parents feel acutely their responsibility for bringing up their
children, but for royal parents the anxiety is trebled. They have to
teach their children to be public figures, as well as civilised human
beings, and they have to achieve both these ends in the unnatural
surroundings of a royal court.

Though 108 years separate the births of the first child of Queen Victoria
and the first child of Queen Elizabeth II, many of the principles of royal
upbringing have remained the same. Each generation of royal parents, for
example, has been particularly anxious to protect its children from the
glitter and excitement of court life. Even the licentious Edward VII wanted
to keep his children 'simple, pure and childlike as long as it is possible'.
The regime for each generation was therefore much the same: a regular
routine, sensible clothes, few parties, not too many toys and very dull
meals. 'The royal children were kept very plain indeed,' said Jane Jones,
nurse to Victoria's younger children. 'It was quite a poor living, only a bit
of roast meat and perhaps plain pudding.' A hundred years later Prince
Charles's favourite meal was boiled chicken and rice.

Another preoccupation of royal parents has been that their children
should learn to be thrifty, despite the conspicuous consumption all
around them. Ribbons from Queen Victoria's hats were used again to trim
her daughters' clothes, Princess Elizabeth's dresses were passed on to
Princess Margaret, Prince Charles was sent out to find a dropped dog lead
because, his mother said, 'Dog leads cost money'. At an interview in 1980
Princess Anne explained that economy had been bred into her: 'I was

brought up by my parents and my nanny to believe that things were not to be wasted. All my childhood life. And that lesson does last, there's no question about it.'

Each generation of royal parents has been so concerned to give its children a good religious education that the parents have usually pre-sided over the first Bible lessons themselves. Later on, confirmation has been an important milestone in the lives of each prince or princess, marking the end of childhood, and celebrated with the giving of valuable presents from the godparents. Although royal children have of necessity been raised in the Anglican Church, they have never been encouraged to become narrow-minded. In 1842 Queen Victoria drew up a memorandum on the religious education of the little Princess Royal, which was to set the pattern for succeeding generations:

> I am quite clear she should have great reverence for God and for religion and that she should show that devotion and love our Heavenly Father encourages his earthly children to have for him, and not one of fear and trembling, and that the thoughts of death and an after-life should not be represented in an alarming and forbidding way and that she should be made to know as yet no difference of creeds and not think that she can only pray on her knees and that those who do not kneel are less devout in their prayers.

When the future Edward VIII was born in 1894 Keir Hardie complained: 'From his childhood onward this boy will be surrounded by sycophants and flatterers by the score and will be taught to believe himself as if a superior creation.' It was a danger which all the royal parents have recognised and tried to guard against. There seems to have come a time with every child when they have realised the power of their position and wanted to test it. Vicky, Princess Royal, was a very haughty little girl and would drop her handkerchief for the pleasure of seeing attendants run to pick it up. Even the sweet-tempered Princess Elizabeth would walk to and fro past the Buckingham Palace sentries to keep them endlessly presenting arms. But such outbreaks of pride would always be hastily suppressed by their parents, and they would be insistent on politeness and consideration, particularly to servants.

A strange contradiction has therefore always permeated the lives of royal children, which they must have found bewildering. Though they were on no account to consider themselves superior to other people, they must indeed be so. Morally they have been expected to set an irreproach-able example to their frailer subjects: 'The Prince of Wales is bound to a pure, a simple, and a cleanly life as vigorously as if the obligation were set down in some constitutional pact,' claimed the *Daily News* at the height of the criticism of the future Edward VII. But goodness alone has never been enough. 'The trouble is people expect one to be a genius,' remarked Prince Charles, when he found himself having to acquire the skills of a naval officer at twice the speed of other people. For despite the increasing egalitarianism of our society we have retained a very old-fashioned, fairy-tale idea of what a prince or princess ought to be. Beauty, brains, charm, dignity, conscientiousness are regarded as essential components of satisfactory royalty. If a royal child is fat or dim, lacks grace or dresses badly, scorn and criticism are heaped upon it. This is particularly true of modern times, when debunking royalty is a popular pastime, but the high expectations of public opinion have always been a strain on royal children.

The nineteenth and twentieth centuries have also seen two further stresses affecting the lives of the royal family. The first has been the toppling of many European thrones, bringing home unpleasantly clearly that royalty survives only by the will of the people, and making each sovereign afraid that his own son or daughter will be the last to ascend the throne. The second, more recent, has been the growing power and intrusiveness of the media, reducing royal privacy and providing a loud-speaker for critics. In his childhood the Duke of Windsor recalled wistfully, 'Royalty was never portrayed offguard'.

It is not surprising, therefore, that even before royal children have been old enough to appreciate their fate, their parents and attendants have viewed their upbringing with anxiety. The sensible Lady Lyttelton, governess to young Edward VII, wrote earnestly: 'Often indeed is my heavy burden increased to a crushing weight when I think of that child.' When the boy was older, his tutors had to give a report *every day* to his parents so not the smallest childish peccadillo passed unnoticed. The next two generations usually escaped with a report once a week, but it was not until the childhood of the present Queen and her sister that the intense scrutiny of performance was dropped. This was partly because, until the Abdication, Princess Elizabeth was not expected to succeed to the throne and partly because of the unusually relaxed attitude of her parents. 'No one could have had employers who interfered so little,' wrote her governess, Marion Crawford. In modern times the Queen and her husband have not taken school reports too seriously: 'Just stay in the middle, that's all I ask,' Prince Philip has told his children.

When royal children do begin to realise their future role, they are confused by the contrast between their very ordinary selves and their exalted position. They find themselves, as George v was told at his confirmation, 'placed from the very first, by the mere accident of birth, in a position which the noblest and most powerful intellects, even when most fortunate, cannot reach through a long life of laborious self-denial'. They realise that to live up to this role they should be beautiful, good and clever, and feel their lack of any of these attributes much more acutely than other children. 'I am not clever, not a bit above average,' the young Edward viii confessed perplexedly to Lord Eshèr, while his younger brother (later George vi), always at the bottom of the class, grew up with an inferiority complex he could never quite shake off.

The tutors and governesses of each generation of royal children were all deeply concerned that their charges mixed so little with other children. The lack of competition was thought to slow down their academic work, and the lack of companions left the shy always shy and the bumptious unsuppressed. But the anxiety of royal parents about sending their children away to school was expressed by Queen Victoria, when considering the education of her grandsons Eddy and George: 'I have a great fear of young and carefully brought up Boys mixing with older Boys and indeed with any Boys in general, for the mischief done by bad boys and the things they may hear and learn from them cannot be overrated.' But if the princes really were to be educated with other children, she was concerned that they should mix broadly: 'Care should also be taken to prevent them merely from associating with sone of the Aristocracy; good boys, of whatever birth, should equally be allowed to associate with them to prevent the early notions of pride and superiority of position which is detrimental to young Princes, especially in these days. . . .'

Despite the problems there has been an increasing tendency for royal children to be educated away from home. Eddy and George were sent to the Royal Navy's training school *Britannia* and in due course George v sent his two elder sons into the Navy, too, at the age of thirteen. The two younger were the first princes to go to prep school. Prince Philip behaved as traditionally as George v when it came to educating his sons: Prince Charles went first to his father's old prep school, Cheam, and then to the same public school, Gordonstoun, where both his brothers were also to be sent. Princess Anne was the first princess to go to boarding school.

How successful have been these efforts to bring up royal children away from home? In terms of the children's happiness, one suspects they have not been ideal. To be torn from a cushioned existence behind palace walls and thrust into a mob of young boys has proved traumatic for most of them. And yet, if the trauma had not come then, would it have appeared later when they had to leave the palace schoolroom for the outside world? Princess Elizabeth and Princess Margaret had the happiest and most sheltered of childhoods but it left Princess Elizabeth painfully shy. When considering the upbringing of her eldest son, very like her in temperament, did she perhaps think it was better he should learn to mix at school, however unwillingly, in order to slip more easily into public life later?

After a rather unhappy decade as a schoolboy Prince Charles flowered, almost overnight it seemed, into an assured, amusing, likeable, articulate young man. Does this prove the success of the system or would it have happened anyway? Looking back at royal childhoods since the time of Victoria and Albert, one is struck by how much the child's personality develops independently, despite all the influences of home or school. Prince Albert's educational system proved excellent for his eldest daughter but hopeless for his eldest son; no amount of naval training could put any spine into Prince Eddy, but Prince George became a typical naval officer; Prince Edward, despite all his charm and ability, failed to make the grade as king, while his despised younger brother won the affection and respect of all his people; Princess Elizabeth and Princess Margaret enjoyed exactly the same upbringing but each carried her very different childish characteristics into adulthood. Lord Melbourne once warned Queen Victoria that education could only 'mould and direct' the character, not change it, but looking at the history of our royal families one wonders if it does even that.

The most outstanding achievement of royal parents in the last five generations has been the maintenance of a close family life despite the distractions of state affairs and public engagements. Victoria and Albert set the style with their magical Christmases at Windsor, summer cruises on their yacht *Fairy* and long adventurous autumn holidays at Balmoral. Their successors have followed a similar annual round, keeping their children with them as much as possible, and providing a security within the royal family that protects its members from being too much buffeted by storms outside. Princess Anne said in 1980: 'The greatest advantage of my entire life is the family I grew up in. I'm eternally thankful for being able to grow up in the sort of atmosphere that was given to me . . . the family was always there, the feeling of being in a family, and we are the stronger for it, I think.'

1

Victoria's Nursery

VICKY

BERTIE

ALICE

ALFRED

HELENA

LOUISE

May Albert with her happy live
In gay and sweet content, sirs,
And their wedding day through England be
A day of merriment, sirs.
Oh! may she have a happy reign,
On her subjects never frown, sirs,
But quickly have a son and heir,
To wear Old England's Crown, sirs.

Broadsheet of 1840

WITHIN a few weeks of her marriage Queen Victoria found herself pregnant. She was most displeased. Instead of going out and about with her dearly loved Albert she was forced to take things easily, giving up pleasures like dancing and travelling. She remained in excellent health but she looked ahead with trepidation, for she could not forget the death in childbirth of her cousin Princess Charlotte, daughter of the Prince Regent. In fact, when the child was born on 21 November 1840 there were no complications, though the Queen suffered severely through a twelve-hour labour. 'O Madam, it is a Princess,' said the doctor attending. 'Never mind', came the undaunted reply, 'the next will be a Prince.'

The birth – even of a mere daughter – brought a great improvement in

Prince Albert's position. As the younger son of Duke Ernst of Saxe-Coburg-Gotha, a minor German state, he had not been considered a very splendid match for the Queen and his adopted country received him with scant respect. The Queen, too, though deeply in love, had not involved him in the business of government and Albert was sensitive to his very secondary role. The birth of Victoria, Princess Royal, changed all that. When her name was introduced into the litany, Albert's was too, an acknowledgment of his part in the founding of a new royal family. Furthermore the distractions of pregnancy had forced the Queen to share some of her work with him and after the birth she came to rely on him increasingly in political and domestic affairs.

On their first wedding anniversary the Princess Royal was christened in the throne-room of Buckingham Palace. The most doting godparent was King Leopold of Belgium, uncle to both Victoria and Albert, who had planned their match while they were in their cradles. Prince Albert had a great sense of occasion and had arranged for the baby to be carried in to the strains of a chorale he had himself composed. But the late arrival of the Duke of Wellington spoiled the plan, for instantly the choir broke off in the middle of the chorale and launched into 'See the conquering hero comes'. Despite this setback the baby was duly christened with Jordan water from a golden font. The christening cake, designed by Albert, showed Neptune beside Britannia, who carried a baby princess in her arms.

In fact it was more often Albert who danced the baby on his knee. 'He makes a capital nurse,' Victoria wrote to her uncle, '(which I do not, and she is much too heavy for me to carry), and she already seems so happy to go to him.' Albert was delighted with his little daughter and most anxious for her welfare. When the court travelled to Windsor for the baby's first Christmas he carried her all the way himself and constantly looked out for patches of ice or potholes in the road. Indeed the royal parents were so protective that rumours began to spread that there was something wrong with the baby (as they were to do with Princess Margaret nearly a century later). In the summer of 1841, however, the Princess began to be driven out in a carriage every morning, in a white muslin dress and Quaker bonnet, clapping her hands with delight at the enthusiastic crowds. The rumours swiftly vanished.

The Queen at first took a rather detached interest in her baby. She saw her twice a day and occasionally watched her being bathed but she showed no desire to do it herself. Breast feeding she never considered for a moment; the very idea was repugnant to her. Indeed she disliked the

The christening of the Princess Royal in the throne-room of Buckingham Palace, 1841, by C. R. Leslie.

The Prince of Wales aged five months with his sister, the Princess Royal; after a painting by Sir W. Ross.

whole business of childbearing which she saw as 'the shadow-side of marriage' and 'such a complete violence to all one's feelings of propriety (which God knows receive a shock enough in marriage alone)'. She also had no particular love for small babies: 'An ugly baby is a very nasty object – and the prettiest is frightful when undressed – till about four months; in short as long as they have their big body and little limbs and that terrible frog-like action.' She was therefore somewhat indignant when her uncle Leopold, soon after the birth of the Princess Royal, looked forward to seeing her with a large family. She wrote back:

I think, dearest Uncle, you cannot *really* wish me to be the 'Mamma d'une *nombreuse* famille', for I think you will see with me the great inconvenience a *large* family would be to us all, and particularly to the country, independent of the hardship and inconvenience to myself, men never think, at least seldom think, what a hard task it is for us women to go through this *very often*. God's will be done. . . .

To Victoria's annoyance God willed that in the spring of 1841 she was pregnant once again. On 9 November 1841, only eleven-and-a-half months after the birth of her first child, she produced 'a fine large Boy'. 'My sufferings were really very severe,' the Queen recorded, 'and I don't know what I should have done but for the great comfort and support my beloved Albert was to me during the whole time.' The birth of a healthy prince was received with delight throughout the country. It was the first time in eighty years that a male heir had been born to a reigning monarch, and crowds gathered in the streets, cheering and singing 'God save the Queen'. With customary forethought Prince Albert had ready a brooch of the Prince of Wales crest to give to his wife.

The boy was named after his father and from the beginning was expected to turn out a carbon copy of him. Only a month after his birth Victoria wrote to her uncle Leopold: 'You will understand *how* fervent my prayers and I am sure *everybody's* must be, to see him resemble his angelic dearest Father in *every*, *every* respect, both in body and mind.' Most people long to duplicate themselves in their children; Victoria longed to duplicate Albert, 'such a perfect being', and was to be equally doomed to disappointment.

In the winter of 1841, however, no premonitions of future problems disturbed the parents' pleasure in their son, 'a wonderfully strong and large child, with very large dark blue eyes, a finely formed but somewhat large nose and a pretty little mouth'. On Christmas Eve Albert wrote to his father, 'Today I have two children of my own to give presents to,' and described their 'happy wonder at the German Christmas tree and its radiant candles'.

Unfortunately the happy family Christmas was scarcely over when problems in the nursery led to the first serious quarrel between Victoria and Albert. The household, including the nursery, was under the management of Baroness Lehzen, who had once been Victoria's governess, and still wielded great influence over her. Albert was very jealous of Lehzen's influence and also very concerned about the health of the Princess Royal, who had been thin and weak for several months. In mid January his resentment and anxiety boiled over into a great row, originally over mismanagement in the nursery, but extending, as quarrels have a tendency to do, into the bigger issue of getting rid of Lehzen. In his rage Albert described her as 'a crazy, common, stupid intriguer, obsessed with lust of power, who regards herself as a demi-god'. When the storms of wrath on both sides had subsided, Albert emerged the victor. Lehzen was retired to Germany, the nursery was reformed and the management of all the royal homes came into his capable hands.

Before reorganising the nursery Victoria and Albert consulted Baron Stockmar, who had once been Albert's doctor and was now a highly valued friend and adviser to them both. Although his ideas on education were to prove rather severe, he had some quite modern ideas on the upbringing of children, insisting on vaccination, sensible diet and sunny, airy rooms for the nurseries. He recommended that the superintendent of the nursery should be 'a person of Rank', whom the parents would therefore respect, and 'good and intelligent, experienced in the treatment of children, of good and refined manners, conciliatory and at the same time firm of purpose'. Such a paragon was to be found, he suggested, in the person of Lady Lyttelton, who had been a Lady of the Bedchamber since 1838. Lady Lyttelton was in her fifties, a calm, intelligent, competent woman who fitted easily into court life without ever losing her independence. She was bound to get on well with the Queen for she shared her enthusiasm for Prince Albert, describing him as 'handsome enough to be the hero of a fairy tale – and very like one'. She was not particularly eager to run the nursery, foreseeing the difficulties that might arise, and only accepted under certain conditions. She was to be 'the sole judge of the conduct of those persons who serve under her ... and they all be ordered to consider her as the only Chief to whom alone they can address themselves in all their affairs, their wants, difficulties, contrarieties or disagreements'. Although she would of course obey the royal parents she sought permission 'to ask questions, to discuss doubtful points, and even to maintain her own opinions by argument, without reserve'.

In fact the only serious disagreement between Lady Lyttelton and her employers was whether the children should say their prayers sitting up in bed, as the Queen wished, or kneeling down as the High Church inclinations of Lady Lyttelton preferred. In all other matters Victoria found her 'so agreeable and so sensible'. The nursery became a happy, well-organised place with a considerable staff of nurses, nursery maids and footmen. Lady Lyttelton taught the children their first lessons but later three sub-governesses were also employed. She described her days as occupied with 'accounts, tradesmen's letters, maids' quarrels, bad fitting of frocks, desirability of rhubarb and magnesia, and by way of intellectual pursuits, false french genders, and elements of the multiplication table'.

Threatening letters directed at the children were frequently received and made Prince Albert particularly anxious about the security of the nursery. Every evening he would check all the windows, lock the door and take the key away. In the morning he returned to release the nursery staff and take the children to visit their mother. Victoria took an increasing pleasure in her children, particularly in the Princess Royal who at two years old was already 'quite a little companion', but Albert was the more frequent visitor to the nursery. He once built a house of bricks so tall he had to stand on a chair to finish it, and he would play the organ with a baby bouncing on each knee.

When Lady Lyttelton first took over the nursery, the Princess Royal showed an 'unconquerable horror' at the sight of her, sensing perhaps a will as determined as her own. Little 'Pussy', as her parents called her, had been treated rather like an expensive toy. Dressed in velvet, lace, pearls and diamonds, she would sit on her mother's lap during an audience and extend her hand for a kiss. Lady Lyttelton treated her more like an ordinary child and soon gained her affection. She called her governess 'Laddle' and Lady Lyttelton called her 'Princessy'.

Although the Princess was imperious and self-willed, Lady Lyttelton was captivated by her charm, gaiety and loving nature. 'Yesterday I was playing with her', she wrote to her family, 'when she suddenly took my old head between her tiny hands, and very gently kissed my forehead, before I knew what she was about, and then laughed most slily. It was just as her mother does to her; the very drollest little compliment.' The Princess was often naughty – she once bit her governess's hand – but it was difficult to remain angry with such an engaging personality. Once, after playing up for an hour, she asked to speak to Lady Lyttelton: 'I expect her usual penitence, but she delivered herself as follows: "I am very sorry, Laddle, but I mean to be just as naughty again."'

However much Lady Lyttelton tried to maintain a sensible routine for the Princess Royal, there were always interruptions to unsettle her. 'I do wish,' she wrote, 'that all her fattest and biggest and most forbidding looking relations, some with black bushy eyebrows, some with staring distorted, short-sighted eyes, did not always come to see her all at once and make her naughty and her governess cross. Poor little body! She is always expected to be good, civil and sensible. . . .' There were also expeditions with the Queen and Prince Albert which produced a real contrast to the peace of the nursery. After driving to Walmer Castle in November 1842 Lady Lyttelton described

the immense crowds, the continual cheers, the fright less we should smash hundreds at every turn, and all the excitement of wreaths and bonfires, and triumphal arches, church bells and cannons, all the way along we kept flying and dashing, escort panting, horses foaming and carriages swaying with the speed. The children will grow up under the strangest delusion as to what travelling means, and the usual condition of the people, in England! They must suppose one always finds them shouting and grinning and squeezing, surrounded by banner and garlands.

The return home was less glamorous. The Queen, Lady Lyttelton and the children arrived back at Windsor to find the head nurse taken sick and 'all our little possessions, night things, play things, *rusks*, shawls, etc.' left behind, as well as the nurse maid. So Lady Lyttelton, helped by the Queen,

had the sole charge of Princey and Princessy, who were taken with tearing spirits, and a rage for crawling, climbing, poking into corners, upsetting everything, and after a little while being tired, cross and squally for hours, till gradually the most necessary absentee people and things dropped in, and I, more untidy and horrid than a beggar, but easy about the children, came up *home* at last and enjoyed the great luxury of a nice fire and drawn curtains. . . .

On 25 April 1843 Victoria gave birth to Princess Alice, who was to be the great grandmother of Prince Philip, Duke of Edinburgh. Although both Houses of Parliament sent 'addresses of congratulation and condolence' because the baby was not a boy, her parents and brother and sister were delighted with her and soon gave her the nickname Fatima because she was such a bouncing baby.

In May the whole family travelled to Claremont to spend the Queen's birthday there. Prince Albert was tremendously good at organising these special occasions. On the day itself he arrived at the nursery at eight o'clock, looking very dashing in a many-coloured dressing gown, and took the children off to the Queen. The Princess Royal looked bewitching in a muslin frock embroidered with lilies of the valley and rosebuds, and the baby had a small bunch of flowers for her Mama. Prince Albert had arranged the Queen's presents under a magnificent bower of flowers in her breakfast room. In pride of place was a picture of baby Alice by Landseer, secretly commissioned by Prince Albert, which showed her lying in an old Saxon cradle watched over by Dandie, the black terrier.

This charming idea was typical of the consideration and affection which Albert showed towards his wife. When she was pregnant he wheeled her from room to room, and allowed no one to lift her but himself; during the birth of their children he was beside her all the time. In the evenings he would read to her while she sat sewing or they would entertain each other with singing and piano playing. 'Oh! what a blessing it is that "Love rules the court" as he does!' wrote Lady Lyttelton. 'What a mine of blessings there is, all sent thro' those potent blue eyes.'

After three years of marriage Victoria had come to revere and adore her husband. It was not just a sexual passion, though that doubtless played a part, but an appreciation of the 'mine of blessings' he had brought her. Albert has been accused of turning Victoria from a laughing girl into a sober matron but she herself was delighted with her new intellectual interests and her growing preference for the peace of the country to the bustle of the town. Fourteen years later she explained in a letter to her eldest daughter just what her marriage to Albert had meant to her.

I had led a very unhappy life as a child – had no scope for my very violent feelings of affection – had no brothers and sisters to live with – never had a father – from my unfortunate circumstances was not on a comfortable or at all intimate or confidential footing with my mother (so different from you to me) – much as I love her now – and did not know what a happy domestic life was! All this is the complete contrast to your happy childhood and home. Consequently I owe everything to dearest Papa. He was my father, my protector, my guide and adviser in all and everything, my mother (I might almost say) as well as my husband. I suppose no-one ever was so completely altered and changed in every way as I was by dearest Papa's blessed influence.

In many ways, of course, Victoria's devotion to Albert was a good thing for their children. Although she was the Queen, there was no doubt that he was head of the family and the children grew up in a secure and loving atmosphere which set a pattern for family life in Victorian times. A few weeks after the birth of her fourth child, Alfred, in 1844, Victoria wrote

Princess Alice in the Saxon cradle, by Landseer. The painting was specially commissioned by Prince Albert as a birthday present for the Queen.

proudly to uncle Leopold about gratifying articles in the press: 'They say *no* Sovereign *was more* loved than I am (I am bold enough to say), and *that*, from our *happy domestic home* – which gives such a good example.' But Victoria's implicit faith in Albert's perfection had disadvantages too. It meant she rarely allowed her maternal feelings to soften his sometimes stern attitude towards the children and – worse still – made her constantly disappointed because they were not turning out as wonderful as their father. *'None* of you,' she wrote, 'can *ever* be proud enough of being the *child* of such a father who has not his *equal* in this world – so great, so good, so faultless. Try . . . to follow in his footsteps and don't be discouraged, for to be *really* in everything like him *none* of you, I am sure, will ever be.'

Of course they were discouraged, particularly Bertie, the Prince of Wales, who was judged as 'sadly backward' by the Queen before he was a year old. Lady Lyttelton had a much higher opinion of him than his parents did. She described him, at two years old, as 'backward in language' but otherwise 'very intelligent and generous and good tempered, with a few passions and *stampings* occasionally; most exemplary in politeness and manner, bows and offers his hand beautifully, besides saluting *à la militaire* – all unbidden.' A few months later she held him on her lap during a military review and was charmed by his reaction to the firing. 'I afraid! Soldiers go popping! No more! I cry!' he said to her, but 'conquered himself completely, did not cry a drop, and grew quite calm before it ceased.'

It was the greatest misfortune for Bertie that his elder sister was so very bright. He appeared more backward than he was by comparison with her and it offended his parents' sense of what was fitting that the heir to the throne should be so outshone by a girl. How often they must have said to themselves, 'If only Vicky were a boy'.

By the age of six the Princess Royal was already becoming too much of a handful for Lady Lyttelton and a governess was engaged for her called Miss Hildyard, a clergyman's daughter. She made rapid progress and her tantrums grew rarer as she became absorbed in her studies. When she was seven Lady Lyttelton observed that she 'might pass (if not seen but only overheard) for a young lady of seventeen in whichever of her three languages she chose to entertain the company'. Soon she was studying Gibbon and Macaulay with Dickens, Shakespeare and George Eliot for light relief. The Queen encouraged her gift for drawing and they would sit side by side in front of their easels, the Princess on a pile of cushions. She also learned the piano but disliked practising and preferred to sit next to her father at the organ, turning the pages and listening to him play.

'Tender Annuals', a satirical print by W. Kohler on the regular additions to Prince Albert's nursery.

A popular print, c. 1849, of the royal family at Windsor. Prince Alfred and his four sisters admire the Prince of Wales's rowing; unfortunately little admiration ever came his way in real life.

The Prince of Wales probably realised from an early age that he was not as clever as his sister and this discouraged him from using the brains he had. Certainly by the age of five he was 'uncommonly averse to learning' and exhausted Lady Lyttelton's patience with his 'wilful inattention and constant interruptions, getting under the table, upsetting the books and sundry other *anti-studious* practices'. He began to stammer and the Princess Royal teased him about it, enraging him. He could not even lord it over his younger brother and sister for by the age of six he had been overtaken in his lessons by Princess Alice. His mother frequently referred to him as 'poor Bertie'.

When he was seven the Prince of Wales was handed over to the care of a tutor, thirty-year-old Henry Birch, who had been a master at Eton. Birch found his royal pupil 'extremely disobedient, impertinent to his masters and unwilling to submit to discipline'. He was selfish, over-sensitive and given to uncontrollable rages. Birch blamed this partly on the lack of companions of his own age to rub his corners off and partly because he was so often 'the centre round which everything seems to move'. For though his schoolroom life was austerely simple, there were enough formal occasions to give Bertie a high sense of his own importance. In September 1846, for example, he accompanied his parents on a cruise down the coast of Devon and Cornwall and was made a great fuss of, particularly when he appeared in his sailor suit for the first time. 'The Navy is delighted. God bless our little Admiral,' read the commander-in-chief's signal at the end of the voyage. At a state visit to the City of London two years later he was greeted as 'the pledge and promise of a long race of Kings' and the gentleman deputed to serve him wine at lunch shed tears at the sight of him and had to leave the room. It must have been very confusing for a young boy to be so fêted and respected outside his family and regarded as such a disappointment within it.

The royal nursery was still filling up. Princess Helena was born in 1846 and Princess Louise in 1848. While she was expecting Louise the Queen suffered great anxiety over the revolutions toppling her fellow monarchs in Europe, and she prophesied that as a result Louise would be 'something unusual' which indeed she was. While Helena grew up to be a plain, dull and dutiful daughter, Louise was pretty, gay, very artistic and so undutiful that in adult life she was rarely invited to visit her mother. As a baby, though, she was placid and happy and much petted by her older brothers and sisters.

The 1848 revolutions had a sobering effect on Victoria's plans for her children and she resolved: 'Let them grow up fit for *whatever station* they

The Swiss Cottage in the grounds of Osborne House on the Isle of Wight.

The royal children's gardening tools, still preserved at Osborne.

may be placed in – *high or low*.' Her guiding principle she had laid down in a memorandum: 'That they should be brought up as simply as possible and that they should be as often as possible with their parents (without interfering in their lessons) and place their greatest confidence in them in all things.' Prince Albert believed that physical punishment was sometimes necessary to teach obedience (though the girls were usually confined to their rooms instead) but there was no cruelty in the royal nursery and no punishment was permitted without the parents' consent.

To live to the full the ideal family life they both delighted in, Victoria and Albert longed for a private home, more intimate than Windsor and more secluded than Buckingham Palace. Their choice fell upon Osborne House on the Isle of Wight. Albert pulled down the Georgian house and designed a large villa in Italian style, which they first visited in 1846.

Osborne became a children's paradise. There was the beach to bathe from, two thousand acres to walk and ride in, yachting excursions along the coast and thrilling views of ships sailing in and out of Portsmouth. Prince Albert imported from Germany a prefabricated Swiss Cottage with its own kitchen and grocer's shop. Here the children learned to clean and cook and entertained visitors to tea. The boys also learned carpentry and there was a miniature fort on which they could practise their military strategy. To encourage them to cultivate their own gardens, the children were given a set of miniature tools with their own initials. Albert may have been a strict father but he was also an imaginative one and, only twenty-nine when Louise was born, he had not forgotten what it was like to be a child. He wanted for them the happy childhood he had enjoyed, but he wanted from them the same earnestness and application that he had shown. The failure of his eldest son to match up to this expectation was to cast a faint shadow over the next decade of family life.

2

Sunshine and Shadow

VICKY

BERTIE

ALICE

ALFRED

HELENA

LOUISE

ARTHUR

LEOPOLD

BEATRICE

Here's to the Queen and Albert gay
And all the children too, hurray
May another come the first of May
For another royal christening.

Ballad of 1850

THE 1850s opened happily for the family of Victoria and Albert with the birth of a third son on 1st May. 'A fine fat Prince of the blood royal is added to the nursery', wrote Lady Lyttelton, who now had seven children under her care. Victoria had planned to call the child after the grand old Duke of Wellington, the hero of Waterloo, and by a happy coincidence little Arthur was born on the Duke's eighty-first birthday. The Duke said the naming of the Prince gave him more pleasure than all his military decorations.

Arthur slept in the same carved wooden cradle as his brothers and sisters had before him and wore the same beautiful christening robe. In a chorale written specially for the christening Prince Albert expressed a typically Victorian view of the precious innocence of childhood:

Sunshine and Shadow

In life's gay morn, e'er sprightly youth
    By vice and folly is enslaved
Oh may thy Maker's glorious name
    Be on thy infant mind engraved!
So shall no shades of sorrow cloud
    The sunshine of thy early days,
But happiness in endless round
    Shall still encompass all thy ways.

A polite, fair-haired, comely boy, Arthur was to be one of his mother's favourite children, the only one of her sons not to give her great anxiety. Surprisingly for such a sweet-natured child, 'so gentle, so dear, so good' as a lady-in-waiting described him, Arthur always wanted to be a soldier. It was no doubt the influence of the Duke of Wellington, who when his godson was only two, showed him all over Apsley House on the thirty-seventh anniversary of Waterloo. The Duke died soon after, but Arthur always retained a great admiration for him. In plays and charades he invariably chose to be a military character and at three years old he dressed up as a Scots Fusilier to have his portrait painted. When he was older he collected mementoes of the Iron Duke and studied his campaigns.

Arthur was the last royal baby to come into Lady Lyttelton's care for when the death of her daughter left her with four motherless grandchildren to look after, she prepared to leave her royal charges. At New Year 1851 she watched the children dancing for the last time. The Prince of Wales did the Highland Fling, 'active and nimble and in such *perfect* time'. A fortnight later she left Windsor. 'The darlings all came up in succession, and a bad spot of road it was to get through. . . . The children all cried and were most touching. The Prince of Wales, who has seen so little of me lately, cried and seemed to feel most. . . . Princess Alice's look of soft tenderness I never shall forget, nor Prince Alfred with his *manly* face in tears looking so pretty. . . .'

Lady Caroline Barrington, a sister of Earl Grey, took over the supervision of the nursery with a host of helpers to attend to the children's every need. Several nurses watched over the babies and as soon as they began lessons, at three or four, they learned English from Miss Hildyard, French from Madame Rollande de Sange, German from Fraulein Gruner and music from Mrs Anderson. When the boys reached about eight they passed into the care of governors or tutors. Miss Sherett looked after the girls' clothes and Monsieur Nestor their hair. While still very young they were taught to ride and to dance, and at Osborne

'The First of May' by Winterhalter, 1851. The Duke of Wellington presents a gift
to his godson Prince Arthur, born on the Duke's birthday and named after him.

Prince Arthur and Prince Leopold, from one of Queen Victoria's sketchbooks.

they had swimming lessons in a sort of floating bath devised by Prince Albert.

In consultation with Baron Stockmar their parents had devised for them a full and varied education, with special emphasis on languages, which was fortunate as all but Louise were to make foreign marriages. Even Bertie, the black sheep, became extremely fluent in French and German. The children worked six days a week and there were no regular holidays, but feast days, family occasions, movements around the royal homes and special treats gave them plenty of light relief. In fact they were not so much overworked as over-watched. Every minute of the day was planned for them, both work and play. Brothers and sisters were never left alone together in the same room and they only mixed with the children of the aristocracy on formal occasions such as children's balls. When a few hand-picked Eton boys were invited to Windsor to meet the Prince of Wales, youthful chatter was inhibited by the unbending countenance of Prince Albert, who found it very difficult to relax with strangers, though he could be great fun in the bosom of the family.

Indeed when Prince Frederick William of Prussia came to visit the Great Exhibition of 1851 what impressed him most about the English princes and princesses was their relaxed and affectionate family life. Although he was twenty he was thrown a great deal into their company because Prince Albert had long since picked him out as a possible husband for the Princess Royal, then only ten. With perfect confidence she conducted him around the exhibition, and was later enraged to be told she was too young to go to the opera with the royal party. Although no word of a possible marriage was breathed to her, Vicky was far too bright not to realise what was in the air, and after Frederick had left she exchanged affectionate letters with him from time to time.

The Prince of Wales had accompanied his parents to the splendid opening of the Great Exhibition at Crystal Palace but he disgraced himself by preferring the waxworks of the Thugs of India to anything else. This seems a perfectly natural preference for a nine-year-old boy, but to Prince Albert it was yet further proof of the stupidity of his eldest son.

It was a tragedy for Bertie that he was the heir to the throne. As a younger son he would have been loved for his affectionate nature and his lack of intellect would have been overlooked. But as it was, those dealing with him were trying to mould him into their vision of the perfect king, a man 'of calm, profound, comprehensive understanding, with a deep conviction of the indispensable necessity of practical morality to the welfare of the Sovereign and People'. Victoria's attitude to her son was further influenced by two contrasting images in her mind: one was the perfection of beloved Albert, the other the notorious imperfections of her Hanoverian uncles, particularly the Prince Regent. She successfully suppressed most of her fun-loving Hanoverian characteristics on her marriage to Albert and she was determined to stop them reappearing in her son and heir. She therefore acquiesced in the very strict educational routine to which the Prince of Wales was subjected.

In 1852 it was decided a tougher tutor might get more work out of Bertie and the amiable Mr Birch was replaced by Frederick Gibbs, a grey humourless bachelor of twenty-nine. Bertie had eventually become very fond of Birch and was much upset by his departure. Lady Canning, a lady-in-waiting, wrote: 'It has been a trouble and sorrow to the Prince of Wales, who has done no end of touching things since he heard he was to lose him . . . his notes and presents which Mr Birch used to find on his pillow were really too moving.'

But Bertie never came to like Gibbs and showed this in his behaviour. An entry in Gibbs's diary reads: 'A very bad day. The P. of W. has been like a person half silly. I could not gain his attention. He was very rude, particularly in the afternoon, throwing stones in my face.' On another occasion: 'During his lesson in the morning he was running first in one place, then in another. He made faces, and spat. Dr Becker complained of his great naughtiness. There was a great deal of bad words.' (One wonders how, in such a sheltered childhood, the Prince had ever learned any bad words.)

Dr Becker, who taught the Prince German, thought his rages were due to an overtaxing timetable. 'After every exertion of *at most* one hour, a short interruption of, perhaps, a quarter of an hour ought to be made to give rest to the brain.' Dr Voisin, the French tutor, agreed with Becker and thought Bertie would get worn out early by too much studying. 'Make him climb trees! Run! Leap! Row! Ride!' he advised the royal parents.

But Albert, Victoria and Stockmar could not but believe that the more hours Bertie put in the better the results would be. They viewed his backwardness with compassion, and modified their educational plan to allow for it, but they could not understand or accept his complete lack of effort, or of interest in anything but clothes. Victoria and Albert had started out with good intentions, determined to show great confidence in their heir and initiate him early into the affairs of state but his appalling behaviour changed their plans. He was to be admonished, protected, treated as a child, until some improvement took place.

In his early teens he studied from eight am to seven pm including

Saturday. In addition to languages he was taught social economy, algebra and geometry, chemistry and Latin. He was taken to Faraday's lectures at the Royal Institution and to a Latin play, neither of which he could have understood in the slightest. His activities included riding, gymnastics, dancing, army drill, swimming, skating and croquet. It was a good, broad education, but there was too much of it.

In later years, though, the Prince of Wales was to stress that he had always loved his parents, despite their strictness, and that he had many happy memories of his childhood. Victoria and Albert were imaginative in the diversions they provided for their children and they spent a lot more time with them than most upper class parents would have done at that time. They were taken to the zoo and the pantomime, to the circus and the opera, and were entertained at home by conjurers, actors and singers. They went for walks and drives, picked fruit, flew kites, played skittles, collected natural specimens, cooked meals in the Swiss Cottage, all in the company of their ever-loving, ever-anxious parents.

To improve their minds and their confidence, and for sheer fun, they were encouraged from the earliest age to entertain the household with music, recitation and acting. They were taught to perform in French and German, as well as English, and when Bertie was only ten and Vicky eleven they acted scenes from Racine's *Athalie*. On Bertie's thirteenth birthday he performed a scene from *Henry VI*, Vicky declaimed the whole of Shylock before the court, and Alfred recited the fable of the Fox and the Crow. 'The little ones did their part likewise, and very well too,' Albert wrote proudly afterwards.

Earlier that same year, 1854, the children had acted together a dramatisation of 'The Four Seasons' for their parents' wedding anniversary. Princess Alice entered first as Spring, scattering flowers and reciting verses; then came Vicky and Arthur representing Summer (the Queen was shocked by Arthur's scanty attire). Alfred as Autumn wore a panther-skin and a vine-leaf crown and Bertie, covered in icicles, acted Winter with Louise. Finally the Seasons gathered on the stage and Helena, clothed in white and holding a long cross, pronounced a blessing upon her parents. At the end, to complete the family gathering, a nurse brought in the newest baby, Prince Leopold, then ten months old.

The birth of Leopold in April 1853 was quite a milestone in medical history for the Queen was given 'blessed Chloroform' for the first time: 'the effect was soothing, quieting and delightful beyond measure'. It was very enlightened of Albert to encourage the use of chloroform, as at the time many people were still arguing that it was a woman's duty to endure

The Prince of Wales (left), Prince Alfred and Mr Gibbs in February 1854.

without alleviation the pain of childbirth. Victoria's enthusiasm helped to get the treatment publicised and accepted.

Sadly Leopold was not only a very ugly but a very ailing baby. Eventually haemophilia was diagnosed, the horrible bleeding disease which affects only males but is carried on by females. Victoria was particularly outraged by the discovery of haemophilia because it was entirely unexpected; there were no records of any bearers in her family or in Albert's. But Vicky, Alice and Beatrice all proved to be transmitters and through them it was spread into the royal houses of Europe.

Leopold's childhood was inevitably accompanied by much suffering and loneliness. Fortunately he was the cleverest of the princes and could enjoy books during his long periods in bed, but it was a great frustration for him to be out of so many activities and to find himself so often the one to be left behind. Efforts to protect him led to battles, and Lady Augusta Stanley described him as 'a dear, but passionate and always frightfully naughty in the presence of his parents, who think him quite a Turk'. When he was seven, and very ill, his parents had to go to London on business leaving him at Windsor. 'Poor little boy,' Victoria wrote afterwards, 'he was alarmed himself that evening, when he was so exhausted, so restless and cold – but said when Lady Caroline said we must be telegraphed to "Don't alarm dear Mama, lest it should distress her" which showed such thought and affection for so young a child.' The Queen's concern for her youngest son did not soften the brutally frank way she was accustomed to describe her children. She wrote of him at the age of four: 'He is tall, but holds himself worse than ever, and is a very common-looking child, very plain in face, clever but an oddity – and not an engaging child though amusing.' However, as Leopold came to show more and more of beloved Albert's brains Victoria forgave him his ugliness, and eventually he became the 'dearest of my dear sons'.

Soon after they were married Victoria and Albert had paid their first visit to the Scottish highlands, and were immediately enraptured. To Albert the mountains and glens brought back memories of his native Thuringia, while Victoria delighted in the scenery, the unaffected highland people and the distance from the cares of London. They decided after several visits that they must have a home of their own in Scotland and in 1848 they leased Balmoral castle. 'It is a pretty little castle in the old Scottish style' wrote Victoria. 'There is a picturesque tower and garden in front, with a high wooded hill; at the back there is wood down to the Dee; and the hills rise all around.' In 1852 they bought the castle and seventeen thousand acres for the sum of 30,000 guineas. It was an investment which

A tableau of the seasons performed at Windsor in 1854. From left to right: Alice, Arthur, Vicky, Helena, Alfred, Louise and Bertie.

Prince Leopold, the haemophiliac prince, in 1857. His mother described him as 'a very common-looking child'.

was to pay dividends, for each generation of the royal family came to love their Scottish retreat.

Charmed though they were by the cosiness of Balmoral, Victoria and Albert soon found it too small for their growing family. In September 1853 they laid the foundation stone of a new house and all the children signed a parchment which was buried within it. Two years later a much larger castle had risen on the site, romantically enclosed with numerous turrets and battlements. Inside it was so Scottish as to dazzle the eyes. The carpets, curtains and upholstery were all of different tartans, including a new Balmoral tartan in black, red and lavender, designed by Prince Albert.

The whole family flung themselves enthusiastically into the Scottish way of life. The children learned highland dancing and were kitted out in full highland dress, which was passed down from older to younger. Prince Albert went stalking and fishing, often accompanied by his family, and studied an enormous Gaelic dictionary. Victoria took her daughters to visit the cottages of her tenants and they learned for the first time what poverty could mean. During their first visit to the new house news came of the Fall of Sebastopol and a great bonfire was lit on a cairn. Prince Albert woke up Bertie and Alfred and took them out to see the blaze and the excited highlanders dancing and singing round the flames. The following year one of the excitements was a grand ball to celebrate the completion of Balmoral's ballroom, when even Helena and Louise were allowed to join the dancers.

Victoria was quite intrepid when it came to exploring the area around Deeside and as they grew older the children accompanied her on some exciting expeditions. In 1859 Helena and Louise travelled thirty-five miles with their parents, riding nineteen of them through the most glorious and wild scenery. 'The little girls were in great glee the whole time,' recorded Victoria.

In the autumn of 1855 Prince Frederick, 'Fritz', of Prussia paid a visit to Balmoral. Vicky was only fourteen but it was thought time the two young people had another chance to get to know each other. Vicky had still not been told of her parents' fond hopes but she gave the shy Fritz every encouragement and by the fifth day he had fallen in love with her. He told Victoria and Albert that it was his dearest wish 'to belong to our family' and he was given permission to speak to Vicky. A few days later as they were riding down the slopes of Craig-na-Ban he pressed white heather into her hand and declared his love. When they got back to Balmoral Vicky rushed to tell her mother the momentous news. 'They are ardently

A sketch by the Princess Royal 'For dear Mama' in 1857.

in love,' Prince Albert wrote to Stockmar, and he and Victoria basked in relief that this union, so long desired, was to be a love-match. Was Vicky, at fourteen, really in love with a man she scarcely knew, or was she in love with the idea of being one day Empress of Germany? It is impossible to tell. Certainly they were to remain utterly devoted to each other through all the trials of their later life.

It was agreed that Vicky would not be married until she was seventeen and the next two-and-a-half years were spent rapidly turning her from child to woman. Now she was only allowed to dance with princes but she did have the consolation of frequently dining with her parents in the evening. When she was fifteen she was prepared for her confirmation – a very solemn occasion in Victorian times, marking the putting away of childish things. She also attended her first drawing-room, her tiny figure dwarfed by feathers and train.

Queen Victoria found it very difficult to adapt to her daughter's changed status. She was still deeply in love with Prince Albert and could not welcome the intrusion of a daughter into their precious hours alone. She got on very well with her children while they were young enough to be treated as toys but not so well when they began to develop minds of their own. She wrote in 1856 to Princess Augusta of Prussia:

I find no special pleasure or compensation in the company of the elder children ... and only exceptionally do I find the rather intimate intercourse with them either agreeable or easy. You will not understand this but it is caused by various factors. Firstly, I only feel properly *à mon aise* when Albert is with me, secondly I am used to carrying on my many affairs quite alone; and then I have grown up all alone, accustomed to the society of adult (and never with younger) people – lastly, I cannot get used to the fact that Vicky is almost grown up. To me she seems the same child, who has to be kept in order and therefore must not become too intimate.

Her attitude to Vicky was probably tinged with jealousy, for in his eldest daughter Albert found an intellectual companionship that neither his wife nor his eldest son could provide. From the time of the engagement Prince Albert devoted two hours of his crowded day to preparing her for her future role. His greatest dream was that through this marriage his own liberal ideas would be transplanted into Prussia and influence the course of German history. It was through no fault of Vicky (or Fritz) that this did not happen, for she was born with a natural genius for politics, according to Baron Stockmar, and eagerly absorbed everything Albert taught her. 'From dear Papa I learn more than from anyone else in the world,' Vicky wrote to Fritz, and Albert comforted himself that she would 'go well prepared into the labyrinth of Berlin'.

Vicky's brothers were beginning to grow up too and in 1856 Alfred and Bertie were separated as it was felt the difference in their ages and capacities was disturbing their education. Alfred, known as Affie, was now twelve. He had always wanted to go into the Navy, and though he was destined eventually to succeed his uncle as Duke of Saxe-Coburg and Gotha, his parents were quite willing to let him have a career in the Navy meanwhile. He was sent to live in the Royal Lodge, Windsor, with an engineer officer to tutor him in suitable subjects. The next year he was sent to a house near Portsmouth so that he could go every day to the training ship *Illustrious* for seamanship and navigation. By August 1858 he was ready for a three-day entrance exam, and passed well. Albert was particularly delighted by Alfred's achievement because of his disappointment with Bertie, and he sent the exam papers to the prime minister, Lord Derby, who gratifyingly replied that if Her Majesty's ministers were forced to sit such a paper, 'it would very seriously increase the difficulty of forming an administration'.

Bertie, on the other hand, was still a problem. When the family went to Balmoral in 1856 he was left at Osborne to pursue his studies, but with no noticeable improvement. His father, anxiously reading Bertie's essays and the diary he was forced to keep, was in despair over the lack of imagination, or grammar, or understanding. One essay began: 'The war of Tarrentum, it was between Hannibal the Carthaginian General and the Romans, Hannibal was engaged in a war with it, for some time. . . .' Albert did recognise that Bertie was showing a talent for social life but this merely added to his fears for his son. When Albert was a boy he had written in his diary that he intended to 'train myself to be a good and useful man' and if he was ever naughty he was instantly quelled merely by a 'grave look'. No wonder he could not understand the tantrums and idleness of his eldest son, who would torment his valet and spread black all over a housemaid's dress. One of the few highlights of his early teens for Bertie was the state visit to Paris in 1855. He was enchanted by the gaiety of the people, the beauty of Empress Eugénie, the splendid fireworks at the Versailles ball. At the end of the visit he begged the Empress to let him and Vicky stay on for a few days. She tactfully said that his parents could not do without them but Bertie replied: 'Don't fancy that, for there are six more of us at home, and they don't want us!'

Bertie's favourite among the brothers and sisters left in England was

Princess Alice. Although he admired the Princess Royal he was too aware of her intellectual superiority to get close to her. Alice on the other hand was eighteen months younger than him, and had a much sweeter nature than her elder sister. She showed more sensitivity to suffering than either Vicky or Bertie and at Balmoral spent a lot of time visiting the cottages of the poorer tenants. She was very attached to the Prince of Wales and carried his hair in a locket. Whenever they were apart, as children or adults, they would correspond, and Alice frequently had to smoothe the relationship between Bertie and his parents.

In April 1857 Queen Victoria gave birth to her ninth and last child, Princess Beatrice. On the next day Albert wrote to Princess Augusta of Prussia (Vicky's future mother-in-law):

Mother and baby are doing well. Baby practises her scales like a good prima-donna before a performance, and has a good voice! Victoria counts the hours and minutes like a prisoner. The children want to know what their sister will be called, and dispute which names will sound best, and Vicky says with a sad sigh, 'The little sister will never have known me in the house'.

For Vicky the sands of childhood were running out fast indeed. Her wedding day was fixed for 25 January 1858, two months after her seventeenth birthday. Her parents did all they could to ensure her happiness in Prussia but found the Prussians very arrogant and unsympathetic. All Vicky's ladies-in-waiting were to be German and only after much persuasion from Albert were two young women included. Fritz's parents even wanted the wedding to take place in Berlin but Victoria flatly refused: 'It is not every day that one marries an eldest daughter of the Queen of England. The question therefore must be considered settled and closed.' On the day before the wedding Vicky brought her mother a brooch containing her hair, and told her, 'I hope to be worthy to be your child'. That evening the Queen was overcome by emotion: 'After all, it is like taking a poor lamb to be sacrificed,' she sobbed. For the Princess Royal and her father the worst wrench was yet to come. After a splendid wedding and a brief honeymoon at Windsor, Albert accompanied Vicky and Fritz to Gravesend and took a sad farewell. Back home he wrote to his favourite child: 'My heart was very full when ... you leaned your fore-head on my breast to give free vent to your tears. I am not of a demonstrative nature, and therefore you can hardly know how dear you have always been to me.'

Albert found some compensation for the loss of Vicky in the antics of his youngest daughter, Beatrice, whom he described as 'the most amus-

Princess Beatrice, Victoria's last child, in her cradle at three weeks old.

ing baby we have had'. Victoria gave him a full-size painting of Beatrice by Horsley for his thirty-ninth birthday in 1858 and at Christmas the same year he gave the Queen a marble statue of the princess in a nautilus shell. What charmed the royal parents was that this child was not in the least in awe of them and, because she was the youngest, they allowed themselves to spoil her a little. When told at lunch one day 'Baby mustn't have that, it's not good for Baby,' Beatrice replied, 'But she likes it, my dear' and calmly helped herself. On another occasion she crept up behind her mother and tied her apron strings to the chair on which she sat. The Queen found herself so securely tied that she had to ring for a maid before she could be released. Beatrice was no more frightened of her father than of her mother. When she was four she told Lady Augusta Stanley, 'I was very naughty last night, I would not speak to Papa, but it doesn't signify much.'

Victoria enjoyed writing long and frequent letters to Vicky giving her the minutest details of the family life she had left behind her. On the Queen's birthday at Osborne in May 1858 there took place a family concert which Vicky must have been glad to miss.

After luncheon the children played.
1 Arthur and Alice a little duet.
2 Louise a little piece alone, fairly, but not in time.
3 Alice and Lenchen [Helena] a duet beautifully.
4 Alice and Affie on the violin a little composition of his own – very pretty and of which he is not a little proud.
5 Alice a long, beautiful and very difficult sonata by Beethoven. Arthur recited a German poem, and Lenchen and Louise have something to say – which however has not yet been said.

But the Queen was not wholly satisfied with her birthday celebrations and it was as usual Bertie who disappointed her: 'The only one of all the children, who neither drew, wrote, played or did anything whatever to show his affection – beyond buying for me a table in Ireland – was Bertie. Oh! Bertie alas! alas!'

She found her second son, Alfred, much more agreeable and entertaining than Bertie, and was very upset by Albert's decision in the autumn of 1858 that Alfred should join his first ship. 'Papa is most cruel upon the subject,' she wrote to Vicky. After six weeks' leave at Balmoral Prince Alfred set forth in October to join the frigate *Euryalus* for a voyage to Marseilles, Algiers, Tunis and Alexandria. 'Dearest Affie is gone,' wrote his mother, 'and it will be ten months probably before we shall see his

42

dear face which sheds sunshine over the whole house, from his amiable, happy, merry temper, and again he was much upset at leaving and sobbed bitterly.' It is not surprising that Alfred, only fourteen, felt some trepidation at leaving home, for no special concessions were made to him on board the *Euryalus* and the life of a midshipman must have seemed hard indeed after the tartan comfort of Balmoral.

Bertie too left home in 1858 but only as far as White Lodge in Richmond Park where he was incarcerated with Gibbs and three highly bred young men whose companionship 'away from the world' was to turn him into 'the first gentleman of the country'. Since worldly society and entertainment was what the Prince of Wales loved best, it is not surprising that he did not enjoy his enforced retreat. Things improved when the dreary Gibbs was replaced by Colonel Bruce, but Bertie was still very restricted. Bruce was expected to 'regulate all the Prince's movements, the distribution and employment of his time, and the occupation and details of his daily life'. Even outsiders like Gladstone realised the Prince was being 'kept in childhood beyond his time'.

The reason was of course that Victoria and Albert were still hoping for some miracle to turn him into the paragon they dreamed of. To admit he was grown up would be to admit defeat. Victoria wrote to Vicky in April 1859, when Bertie was seventeen: 'I tremble at the thought of only three years and a half before us – when he will be of age and we can't hold him except by moral power! I try to shut my eyes to that terrible moment! . . . His only safety – and the country's – is his implicit reliance in everything, on dearest Papa, that perfection of human beings.' The Queen seemed to have almost a physical repulsion to her eldest son. His nose and mouth were 'too enormous', his coiffure 'hideous', his legs 'very knockneed' and his face had a 'dull, heavy, blasé look'. She seemed surprised when he put on a colonel's uniform on his seventeenth birthday and looked 'not at all amiss', and then changing into shorts appeared 'not strikingly unbecoming'.

Unfortunately, Victoria's candid nature made her very critical of the children to their face. Preparing to meet Vicky a few months after the marriage she could not resist writing: 'I am very curious to know whether I shall find still some of the old tricks of former times in you? The standing on one leg, the violent laughing – the cramming in eating, the waddling in walking. . . .' To Bertie she could be equally direct and in February 1860 Princess Alice had to soothe him down: 'You must remember she is your mother and is privileged to say such things; and though, as Vicky and I have often and long known, that they are not said in the pleasantest way, and often exaggerated, yet out of filial duty they must be borne and taken in the right way.'

Princess Alice had moved a little more into the limelight with Vicky's departure and it became her turn to spend an hour each day studying with Prince Albert. Although now feeling rather guilty over Vicky's early marriage, and therefore anxious to keep Alice in the background a little longer, Victoria and Albert were already on the lookout for a suitable husband for her. In 1860 Prince Louis of Hesse was invited to Ascot and Alice was as obliging as her sister in falling in love with the chosen one. In November he returned and the engagement was sealed with a kiss, which went straight to the Queen's sentimental heart. 'Such a moment is one most touching and moving to witness for Parents' hearts when 2 such fine and good young beings pour out the first confession of their mutual love.'

A month later the royal family celebrated Christmas at Windsor in traditional style. Ever since Prince Albert first brought over Christmas trees from Coburg in 1841 they had been a major part of the decorations. In each of the Queen's three sitting-rooms the chandeliers were taken down and large trees, covered with candles and bon-bons, took their place. Each member of the family had a table piled high with presents and the younger children would be almost overcome with excitement. Looking at her heap of presents Princess Louise once said it was *'Vraiment un peu trop extravagant'*. In 1860 a baron of beef, 360 pounds in weight, turned for ten hours on a spit and fifty turkeys were cooked as well as a great woodcock pie containing a hundred birds. To the children's delight the lake at Frogmore froze over and they enjoyed skating and ice hockey. Albert was at his most relaxed on these occasions, swinging little Beatrice in a table napkin, pulling her across the ice on a sleigh and joining in all the fun and games with the other children. Happily none of them had a premonition that this was to be their last Christmas with him.

Prince Albert had been overworking for years and in 1861 his health began to deteriorate. The Queen's mother, the Duchess of Kent, died in March and Victoria was so overwhelmed with grief that rumours suggested her mind was affected. The struggle to bring his wife back to normality sapped Albert's strength yet further, and the death of all the Portuguese royal family from typhoid in November added to his depression. Finally he was anguished to learn on the twelfth of the same month that Bertie, now in the army, had enjoyed a brief affair with an actress. When typhoid began to develop a few days later Albert was in no frame of mind to fight back. From the moment he realised he was getting a fever he seemed certain that he was going to die. Princess Beatrice was brought in to try and cheer him up with French verses, and Alice played hymns to him, but gradually he slipped further and further away from his family. On 14 December Louise, Arthur and Leopold were brought in to kiss his hand, but he was unaware of them. The little ones were taken back to the nursery but Bertie, Alice and Helena stayed kneeling by the bedside, watching in misery as their beloved Papa faded quietly away.

With the death of Albert a pall of gloom settled upon the lives of the royal children still at home. 'The whole house seemed like Pompeii, the life suddenly extinguished,' wrote Lady Stanley. Prince Alfred was at sea so it was Arthur who accompanied Bertie at their father's funeral. 'Little Prince Arthur, in a black dress of Highland fashion, walked by his brother's side,' reported the *Daily Telegraph*, 'and the poor little boy sobbed and wept as though his heart would break. It is good for children to weep thus.'

Prince Arthur's grief was not forced. All the children realised the extent of their loss. Though a strict father Albert had been a very affectionate one, and much of the vitality and variety of their family life had sprung from him. When the heart-broken Vicky arrived from Germany she immediately sensed that 'the central point is missing. We wander round like sheep without a shepherd.'

The Queen, who should have been trying to soften the blow for her children, gave way completely to her own sorrow. Instead of comforting them she relied on their total devotion to support her. Bertie promised on Albert's deathbed 'I will be all I can to you', but Victoria could hardly bear to look at him as she considered the worry over his 'fall' had exacerbated Albert's illness. It was upon the eighteen-year-old Alice and the four-year-old Beatrice that the chief burden of the Queen's grief fell. Alice took over the reins of the household and acted as an intermediary with official visitors, while Beatrice received the full force of the Queen's frustrated affections. She wrote to Vicky: 'Sweet little Beatrice comes to lie in my bed every morning which is a comfort. I long so to cling to and clasp a loving being. Oh! how I admired Papa! How in love I was with him! How everything about him was beautiful and precious in my eyes! Oh! Oh! the bitterness of this – of this woe!'

Writing to Vicky three months later she promised to 'strive humbly to do something to make you feel less fearfully the loss of the greatest and best of fathers', but in fact continued to do all she could to keep the children aware of the void in her life and theirs. Tutors were instructed to talk often of 'adored Papa and broken-hearted Mama' and when the Prince of Wales returned from a trip abroad six months after Albert's death his governor was warned that there was to be no 'worldly, frivolous, gossiping kind of conversation. . . . The Prince must be prepared to face in a proper spirit the cureless melancholy of his poor home.'

Fortunately for Alice and Bertie escape from 'cureless melancholy' was in sight, for Victoria was determined to follow Albert's wishes with regard to both their marriages. In July 1862 Alice married Louis of Hesse, though Victoria made sure the occasion was, as she admitted, 'more like a funeral' than a wedding. In March the following year Bertie married Princess Alexandra of Denmark, whose charm and beauty went straight to the hearts of all England, and in particular cheered the forlorn lives of her younger brothers- and sisters-in-law. When Prince Leopold was sent to welcome her on her first visit to Britain he was much exercised over his speech and his bouquet, but found instead he was swept into the arms of this fairy princess and warmly hugged.

Victoria's only pleasure in these days was building memorials to Albert, and the children were inevitably present at sad little ceremonies marking the raising of a stone here or a statue there. They also had to have photographs taken around his bust, even on cheerful occasions like weddings, so that the bride and groom might feel his blessing was upon them. The August visit to Balmoral in 1862 was especially melancholy for it was the Queen's first visit to Scotland without the husband who had shared her deep love for it. She went in a pony chair with her children riding behind her to the summit of Craig Lowrigan where a memorial cairn was to be built. 'Sweet Baby we found at the top. The view was so fine, the day so bright and the heather so beautifully pink – but no pleasures, no joy! All dead!'

Though all the children – even Vicky in Berlin – were never allowed to forget the Queen's misery, Albert's death naturally affected most deeply the lives of the younger children. Eighteen months after his death Alice and Vicky were in Germany with their husbands, Alfred was at sea, and Bertie had been freed by marriage to live an independent life in the social whirl of London. Prince Arthur, now thirteen, also escaped the worst of Victoria's seclusion for he was given his own small establishment at Greenwich under the care of his governor Major Elphinstone, and pleased his tutors with his earnest study. In 1865 he was taken on a tour of the Near East and he spent his fifteenth birthday in Volo Bay. His early devotion to the memory of the Duke of Wellington had never faltered and when nearly seventeen he joined the Royal Military Academy to follow

The mourning children grouped around a bust of Prince Albert. From left to right, Alfred, Alice, Louise, Vicky and Helena.

the career of his hero. The Queen still kept a close watch on his development for she felt that of all her sons Arthur was the one who would wear 'the lily of a blameless life' like the Prince Consort. He was not permitted to go behind the scenes in theatres, or to the Derby, or to wear a centre parting or to put his hands in his pockets, but still his teenage years were freer and more happy than those of his brothers and sisters at this time.

Left at home to share their mother's cheerless life were Helena, Louise, Leopold and Beatrice. Helena and Louise had both suffered from being in the middle of the family. Neither the eldest nor the youngest, nor boys to be trained for a career, they did not perhaps get their full share of attention. Lady Augusta had noted on a visit to Ireland in 1861 that 'Louise was so pleased to be taken a little notice of'. What had brought Louise to the attention of the Irish was her prettiness: Louise was pretty but naughty; Helena (called Lenchen) was good but plain. Louise was not as clever as her elder sisters and had obviously been made aware of this, for on hearing of her father's death she had exclaimed: 'Oh why did not God take me. I am so stupid and useless.' She was, however, the most artistic of the family, and excelled at drawing and painting. Helena was a tomboy, loving riding, swimming and sailing, and more interested in machinery than embroidery. In a letter to Vicky in 1864, when Helena was nearly eighteen and Louise sixteen, Queen Victoria summed up the sisters in her usual blunt manner:

Louise has difficulties to contend with, no doubt – but also great advantages over her sister. She is so handsome (she is so very much admired) and is so graceful and her manners so perfect in society, so quiet and lady-like, and then she has such great taste for art. Poor dear Lenchen, though most useful and active and clever and amiable, does not improve in looks and has great difficulties with her figure and her want of calm, quiet, graceful manners.

On Louise's fifteenth birthday the Queen had written to Vicky: 'These days are so sad now, and yet I wish so much that they should not be so for the children – as Papa was very anxious about that.' In fact she still made little effort to lighten the gloom for her children and was reproachful if they showed any signs of regaining their spirits or enjoying anything. Louise became very close friends with the Princess of Wales but she was never allowed to stay with her in the gaiety of Marlborough House or Sandringham. The elder brothers and sisters were concerned about the life of mourning which the younger ones were forced to share. Princess Alice wrote from Darmstadt of her 'joyous childhood' and added: 'I do feel so much for dear Beatrice and the other younger ones

Princess Beatrice with her nephew, Prince William of Prussia, the future Kaiser, in 1864.

who had so much less of it than we had.' Such hints fell on stony ground.

Helena and Louise had at least enjoyed twelve or so years of the golden age; Leopold and Beatrice, aged eight and four when Albert died, had very few merry years to look back on. For Leopold it was yet another blow in a life which had already proved unkind. Limited as he was by haemophilia, he took some comfort in developing his mind. Had Albert been alive an intellectual companionship could have developed between them and been a mutual delight, but as it was Leopold had only his tutors to talk to after Arthur had gone to Greenwich. Queen Victoria felt her son's illness deeply. She reproached Vicky in 1864 for sending a present only to Beatrice: 'Poor, good Leopold ought not to have been quite forgotten. He suffers so often, and leads so sad and solitary a life. A pretty classical German book would give him much pleasure. . . .' But her concern did not lead her to find him companions of his own age or to cheer his life with amusements.

Beatrice had a great burden to bear. She was 'the only thing I feel keeps me alive' and spent more time with her sorrowing mother than any of the remaining children. Frequently on festive occasions such as weddings the Queen records 'I lunched alone with Beatrice', and one imagines the little girl sadly cut off from the celebrations going on elsewhere. When the Queen travelled, Louise and Helena might be left behind, but hardly ever Beatrice. If she did have to leave 'precious Baby' she insisted that Beatrice should write to her every day with details of her lessons and activities. Her studies followed the same pattern as her sisters, with emphasis on languages and history, but though she was taught to dance there were no more children's balls for her to go to, and when she learned to ride her companion was frequently her mother. Music was her chief accomplishment; she played the piano well and developed a pleasant mezzo-soprano voice.

Living so much in her mother's shadow, Beatrice became something of a shadow herself. The merry, impudent, amusing child became a shy, repressed young girl, scarcely opening her mouth in company. At the age of seventeen she was invited to a ball at Abergeldie Castle but while everyone else was enjoying themselves, she 'sat like a frump all night' because she had the strictest orders only to dance with her brothers. It was not primarily for moral reasons that the Queen was so protective of her. She was selfishly determined to keep Beatrice all for herself as 'no married daughter is any use'. She wrote to Sir Theodore Martin on Beatrice's confirmation at the age of eighteen: 'The Queen can only pray that this flower of the flock (for the Queen may truly say she has never given the Queen one moment's cause of displeasure) may never leave her, but be the prop, comfort and companion of her widowed mother to old age. She is the Queen's Benjamin.' Of course the Queen did not 'only pray'; she gave orders that the subject of marriage was never to be mentioned in front of Princess Beatrice, and when her daughter did, despite her, fall in love with Prince Henry of Battenberg, her mother refused to speak to her for six months.

Princess Beatrice's childhood was cheered to some extent by the frequent visits of her numerous nephews and nieces. Vicky's eldest son Willy (the future Kaiser) was just a few years younger than Beatrice and by the time she was fifteen she was aunt to twenty-one children. The most important of these, to whom the story now turns, were of course the children of the Prince and Princess of Wales.

3

Darling Motherdear

EDDY
GEORGE
LOUISE
VICTORIA
MAUD
JOHN

Twinkle, twinkle little Star,
That's precisely what you are.
Star of England's hopes and mine,
Destined on her throne to shine.

Pretty little royal boy,
Father's pride and mother's joy,
How I long to see thee toddle
And to kiss thy pinky noddle.

Punch, 23 January 1864

WHEN Bertie married Alexandra in March 1863 he was twenty-one and she only eighteen. Delighting in their youth, freedom and a mutual love of society, they danced their way through a whirlwind of a London season. The Queen complained that they were becoming 'nothing but two puppets running about for show all day and night', and prophesied that with such a style of life 'hopes there cannot be'. She managed to depress herself equally with the prospect of their having children, and the fear that they might not. She wrote to Vicky in May: 'though to be sure, unintellectual children which one might fear with B.'s children, would be a great misfortune, it would be very sad if

The Prince and Princess of Wales with their eldest son, Albert Victor, called
'Eddy', in 1865.

they had none, and I sometimes fear they won't. Are you aware that Alix has the smallest head ever seen? I dread that – with his small empty brain – very much for future children.'

On the first count she was soon proved wrong. By the end of June Alexandra was pregnant and shocked her mother-in-law by carrying on with the same hectic way of life. She was at Windsor for the New Year of 1864 and, though seven months pregnant, determined to join the skaters on the Frogmore lake in her sledge chair. She ignored some twinges of pain and enjoyed herself but by the time she got back to Frogmore House she was in labour. No preparations had been made for the event so her lady of the bedchamber, Lady Macclesfield, rushed out to the drapers in Windsor to buy some flannel. A record was kept of the layette so hastily gathered together:

> 2 yards of coarse flannel
> 6 yards of superfine flannel
> 1 sheet of wadding (lent by Mrs Knollys)
> 1 basket (contents wanting)
> 1 superb lace christening robe

There was no time to summon the royal physicians so Lady Macclesfield and the local doctor between them delivered a baby boy at nine o'clock that evening, in the presence only of the Prince. The child weighed scarcely $3\frac{3}{4}$lb but he was healthy. When Lady Macclesfield looked in later to see if the Princess was asleep she found Bertie and Alexandra weeping thankfully in each other's arms.

The Queen decided that the new prince should be called Albert Victor after herself and her husband. Bertie was furious to hear news of this decision from Beatrice before his wishes had even been consulted. However, the Queen got her own way and the baby was christened Albert Victor Christian Edward, though everyone but her called him Eddy. The Queen of course found plenty to criticise at the baptism: 'The poor baby roared all through the ceremony, which none of you did,' she wrote to Vicky. 'Alix looked very ill, thin and unhappy, she is sadly gone off.' The Queen's present to her grandson was a silver statuette of the Prince Consort with an encouraging verse engraved on the plinth:

> Walk, as he walked, in faith and righteousness
> Strive, as he strove, the weak and poor to aid:
> Seek not thyself but other men to bless:
> So win, like him, a wreath that will not fade.

Since the little prince was second in line to the throne his birth inspired some dreadful verses, one beginning 'The night is riven by a new born star'. *Punch* wrote in lighter vein:

> O hush thee, my darling, thy Sire is a Prince
> Whom Mama beheld skating not quite five hours since.
> And Grandpapa Christian is off to the fray
> With the Germans, who'd steal his nice Duchy away.

The Duchy referred to was Schleswig-Holstein, which the Germans did in fact succeed in wrenching from Denmark's grasp. Worry about the Danish reverses slowed Alexandra's recovery from the birth of Eddy, and though she returned to the round of gaiety she was deeply unhappy about her native country. She was determined to take the baby with her to cheer her parents when she visited Denmark in September 1864. Victoria reluctantly agreed but insisted that Eddy should be brought back to her at Balmoral and should not travel on to Sweden. She made it plain that she was determined to interfere in his upbringing as much as she chose: 'Bertie should understand what a strong right I have to *interfere* in the management of the child or children; that he should never do anything about the child without consulting me.'

Queen Victoria loved to be present at the births of her grandchildren but Bertie and Alexandra always managed to avoid this. When a second son was born on 3 June 1865 he was said to be a month premature, but Bertie's brother Alfred had his doubts. 'Pray tell me, it was just at the right time was it not? Mamma and everybody fancied it should only be in July but you told me to expect it just when it did happen. I am sure you said it was later on purpose.' The Queen was also suspicious: 'It seems that *it is not to be* that I am to be present at the birth of your children, which I am very sorry for.'

The baby's other grandmother, Queen Louise of Denmark, read good omens into the premature births of her two grandsons: 'I only hope it is a good sign for their character to be *before* the time in any good impulse of their life and for every good and noble deed.' She was delighted that her daughter had produced a second son and wrote to Bertie: 'How proud you must be, two boys, don't you grow more attached to Alix at every present thus brought to you in pain and anguish.'

Before Queen Victoria could make up their minds for them the Prince and Princess of Wales decided to name the baby George Frederick. The Queen did not approve at all, but she did not press her opposition:

I fear I cannot admire the names you propose to give the Baby. I had hoped for some fine old name. Frederick is, however, the best of the two, and I hope you will *call* him so. *George* only came in with the Hanoverian family.

However if the dear child grows up good and wise, I shall not mind what his name is. Of course you will add *Albert* at the end, like your brothers, as you know we settled *long ago* that *all* dearest Papa's *male* descendants should bear *that* name, to mark *our line*, just as I wish all the girls to have Victoria after theirs.

This last command the parents obeyed, christening the boy George Frederick Ernest Albert, but they resisted calling him Frederick. He was 'Georgie' to his family from babyhood into middle age.

Eighteen months after Prince George was born Alexandra gave birth to a daughter in most unhappy circumstances quite unlike her previous easy confinements. After spending a cold and damp January at Sandringham House she came back to London with a sore throat and painful knee, which were soon diagnosed as rheumatic fever. Five days after her illness had begun she went into labour and suffered great pain for the doctors dared not give her chloroform. When the baby was born on 20 February 1867, and for weeks afterwards, she was far too ill to take an interest in it and looking back always regretted that her eldest daughter had been three months without a mother's care. By the time of the christening in May Alexandra was still too weak to walk and had to be wheeled in to the chapel on her bed. There was the usual dispute about names; the Queen wanted her granddaughter to bear her own name but Alexandra resolutely decided to call her Louise after her mother and her favourite sister-in-law.

Although Alexandra's long illness left her with a permanent stiff leg she was determined not to let it interfere with her activities and by the end of the year she could skate, dance and ride as well as ever. She was also pregnant again. On the 6 July 1868 a second daughter was born and tactfully named Victoria. Despite this compliment the Queen made a great fuss when Alexandra wanted to take her three eldest children on a visit to Denmark that autumn. Anticipating that the Queen would not want her to take Louise, Alexandra wrote a pleading letter:

I must say, that as I am now convinced she is strong and well, I do *not* want to be parted from the little thing . . . I need not tell you, dear Mama, how delighted I am, after nearly *five* years, to return to my parental home and to show them our three eldest children. Oh, what a joy! But it would *break my heart* if I could not take the three children and daily I pray God that *nothing* should arise which would hinder this long hoped-for happiness.

Queen Victoria was not moved. She agreed that the two boys should go but felt Alexandra was selfishly jeopardising Louise's health by wanting

Prince Eddy and Prince George in 1867.

Princess Victoria with her nurse, Mrs Quinlan, in 1869.

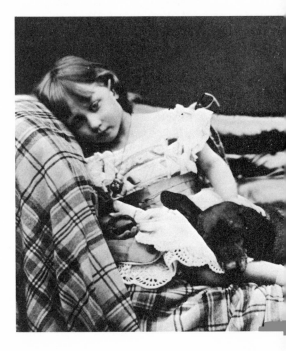

Princess Louise in 1870.

to take her abroad. Bertie wrote back in staunch defence: 'None of us are perfect – she may have her faults – but she is certainly not selfish – and her whole life is wrapt up in her children.' He pointed out with truth that the Queen encouraged Vicky and Alice to bring their children to England every year, so how could she refuse to let Alexandra take her children home to Denmark. The Queen relented. Gradually the Prince and Princess of Wales were going their own way about bringing up their children but not without some damage to their relationship with the Queen. She complained 'Alix and I never will or can be intimate; she shows me no confidence whatsoever, especially about the children.'

The Princess of Wales was to bear two more children. In November 1869 she gave birth to a third daughter, Maud, and seventeen months later came a third son, John. Like her other children John was born prematurely but unlike them he was too weak to survive more than twenty-four hours. His parents were heartbroken. Bertie himself, with tears rolling down his cheeks, placed the body in its tiny coffin and arranged the pall of white satin. His wife watched from her bedroom window as Eddy and George, in grey kilts and black scarves, walked hand in hand with their father in the funeral procession. Alexandra never got over the loss. Eleven years later she wrote to George: 'It is sad to think that nothing remains on earth to remind us of him but his little grave.' Her grief was sharpened by guilt for she felt that if she had rested more in her pregnancy the baby might have survived.

Although the Princess of Wales was only twenty-six there were no more pregnancies. This may have been for reasons of health but it may also have been an indication of the gradual parting of the ways between her and Bertie. Her rheumatic fever had marked a turning point in their relationship. Although they had only been married three years at the time, Bertie had behaved in a most callous way, carrying on his usual amusements despite the fact that his wife lay dangerously ill. Afterwards, though Alexandra overcame the disadvantage of her limp, she could not cover up the increasing deafness which was another legacy of the fever. Nor could she conceal from herself that Bertie was regularly unfaithful, and that all the world knew it. It was a bitter pill to swallow, but she took it with dignity and tolerance, and although she was deeply disillusioned with her husband, a strong affection remained between them. The full force of her love, however, was turned upon her children and upon her favourite home, Sandringham.

This undistinguished mansion seemed a strange choice for the country home of the Prince of Wales. It had, as Lady Macclesfield said, 'no fine trees, no water, no hills, in fact no attraction of any sort or kind'. Yet when it had been enlarged and modernised and filled with comfortable contemporary furniture both Bertie and Alexandra became greatly attached to it. Here, with occasional trips to London, Osborne, Balmoral or Denmark, their children grew up.

Unlike Queen Victoria, Princess Alexandra loved babies. Their nurse later remembered: 'The Princess was in her glory if she could find time to run up into the nursery, put on a flannel apron, wash the children and see them asleep in their beds.' When apart, her letters to the nurse were full of detailed instructions: 'The children must go on with their codliver and steel unless Sir William Jenner sees fit to make some alteration.'

When Prince Eddy was only a fortnight old a nursery footman called Charles Fuller was appointed to watch over him, and in time he became a devoted personal attendant to both the princes. Their nurse, Nanny Blackburn, was so fond of Prince Eddy that she kept his first tooth and set it among turquoises in a ring. They began lessons with a governess but when Eddy was seven and George nearly six they started regular lessons with the Rev. John Dalton, a curate aged thirty-two. He was a man of character and good sense who never hesitated to tell the truth to his employers or to disagree with them over what was best for his pupils. His disciplined puritanism was a useful counterweight to the luxury and self-indulgence of life at Sandringham. In addition to the usual subjects the Princes were taught gymnastics, fencing, riding and shooting, tennis, croquet and football.

The curriculum was much the same as Prince Albert had devised for Bertie, but the whole atmosphere in which the children lived and studied was quite different. This was partly of course because their mother was not the Queen, and so had more time for them, but it was also because that was how their parents wished it to be. Alexandra wanted for them the same simple, loving childhood that she had enjoyed and Bertie was anxious not to repeat his parents' mistakes. He told his mother: 'If children are too strictly or perhaps severely treated they only fear those whom they ought to love.'

The result was five thoroughly spoilt children, viewed with distaste by some of their relations. The three girls who had once been described by Victoria as 'poor frail little fairies' grew into rampaging little girls whom Nanny Blackburn could scarcely control. When the Duke of Devonshire lent Chiswick Park to the Prince of Wales the children scrambled heedlessly over ornamental sphinxes and obelisks and when a gardener protested, kicked him on the shin. When they went to play with other children their hosts hurriedly put away their toys so they should not be broken by the Wales cousins. George was once ordered under the table as a punishment for being naughty in the presence of his grandmother and reappeared amid 'fearful consternation' because he had taken all his clothes off. No wonder Victoria said of these grandchildren: 'Such ill-bred, ill-trained children! I can't fancy them at all.' Alexandra looked on indulgently as her children slid down the stairs on tea trays, rode a pony up into the bedrooms or rang all the service bells at once to bring out the staff. 'They are dreadfully wild,' she admitted to a guest, 'but I was just as bad.'

Alexandra was particularly casual about the education of her daughters. She herself had no intellectual interests and was quite unconcerned when Miss Brown, the governess, reported that Louise, Victoria and Maud could hardly be bothered with books. She made sure they were all taught music, and they learned to dance in the company of their brothers, but their minds were hardly touched by their studies. Apart from being taken on many visits to hospitals they were never taught to play a public role and remained in a childish world of 'Looloo, Toria and Maudie' surrounded by tiny china animals, sea shells and vases. It was unfortunate that they were so close in age for they were invariably treated as a trio, and dressed alike, so it was difficult for individual identities to emerge. Princess Victoria was described by one spectator as '*very* sharp, quick, merry and amusing' but she was given no chance to develop her intelligence. Alexandra wanted her children to stay in a Peter Pan world of perpetual youth and with her daughters she succeeded for a long time. They were in their late teens when they sent drawings of themselves as animals to Francis Knollys, their father's private secretary, with a letter saying, 'We hope the pictures will put you in mind of your little friends Toots, Gawks and Snipey.' Soon afterwards their cousin Princess May was shocked to be invited to a children's party for Louise's nineteenth birthday – 'too ridiculous'.

The Prince of Wales did not take the same detailed interest in his children that the Prince Consort had done. He loved his family dearly and was always ready to take them out for birthday treats, but his continuing search for amusement took him frequently from home. Besides, he was probably aware that it was his infidelities which made Alexandra so possessive of the children and felt that it was only fair to give her a free hand with them. He rationalised this to his mother by saying, 'I think a child is always best looked after under its mother's eye.' He was very disappointed that none of his daughters had inherited their mother's

Princess Alexandra, 'Motherdear', with Eddy (left), George and Louise.

The children of the Prince of Wales playing with the Duke of Teck's children at Chiswick. Prince George, in the centre of the picture, was eventually to marry the girl standing to his right, Princess May. A sketch by Miss Ella Taylor, 1872.

looks. His favourite, Maud, was the prettiest but they all looked rather alike, with high narrow foreheads and protruding eyes.

A much more serious disappointment was the complete lack of progress made by Prince Eddy, the future heir. Before he was a month old Queen Victoria had described him as backward, and for once her pessimism was justified. Eddy was good, gentle and loving but distressingly slow-witted and apathetic. When the Prince of Wales expressed his concern to Mr Dalton, he was reminded that his father had been in despair about him in boyhood. But this can have been little comfort for though Bertie had hated studying he was never stupid, whereas poor Eddy was simply dim in mind and spirit. Bertie found it difficult to be patient with his eldest son, and his endless teasing could not have helped the introverted boy to grow in confidence.

Princess Alexandra was immensely protective of this, the weakest of her flock. She exhorted him to greater effort but always in the kindest way. A letter she wrote to the seven-year-old Eddy in 1871, when Bertie was ill at Sandringham and the children had been sent to their grandmother, shows how different her style of motherhood was to Queen Victoria's. It is impossible to imagine the Queen writing:

> Mama sends a thousand thanks for all the nice little letters, and is so glad to hear from Mr Dalton that Eddy is a good little boy. Mama is so glad dear little Eddy has been going on praying God for dear Papa's recovery and the Almighty God has *heard* our prayers, and darling Papa is going to be quite well again and very soon we hope you may all come home again to see dear Papa once more.

At the time of Bertie's illness Princess Alice's children were also staying with Queen Victoria, and Princess Victoria of Hesse recalled later the fun which the grandchildren had together:

> When we were over the worst of our whooping cough, the Wales cousins and ourselves were moved to Windsor. We were not old enough to understand the anxiety Grandmama was going through when her son was at death's door, and were a very merry party of children. Our wild romps in the great corridor, in which Aunt Beatrice, a girl of thirteen, joined, were often interrupted by one of the pages bringing a message from the Queen that she would not have so much noise. In age, we formed a regular scale, Eddy coming between me and Ella, George between Ella and Irene, while Louise Fife really belonged to the nursery party, Irene, Victoria, Maud and Ernie. Our greatest ambition, when we were with the Wales cousins, when no nursery dragon was in the room, was to steal lumps of sugar from the nursery store and melt them in the lighted candles. The result was burned fingers, an awful smell of burning wax – and no caramel.

Princess Alexandra with, from left to right, Eddy, George, Louise, Victoria and Maud.

There were lovely corners and curtains behind which one could hide and leap out in the dark. Outside the Queen's room there was always a table with lemonade and water, and a dish of biscuits which we used to pilfer.

Bishop Wilberforce, who met both the Wales boys at this time, kindly interpreted Eddy's apathetic gaze as 'that inward look of melancholy which the Prince had'. But the younger brother, he noted, was 'full of fun and spirit and life'. It is difficult to imagine the rather stern figure of George v as 'a jolly little pickle' but in his youth everyone who knew him was attracted by his high spirits. He loved the annual family carnival at his grandparents' home at Fredensborg and his cousin Olga, daughter of Tsar Alexander III, remembered how he would teasingly invite her to 'come and roll with me on the ottoman'. It became a family joke which, when they grew up, he would repeat to her at formal banquets, causing her great discomfiture.

George was so much cleverer than Eddy that he not unnaturally developed a tendency to be over-pleased with himself. When he was eleven Dalton wrote in his record book: 'Self-approbation enormously strong, becoming almost the only motive power in Prince George. . . . The slightest difficulty discourages him and when he frets he finds it hard to subdue himself.' On the whole though, despite the difference in their position and their abilities, the two brothers got on extremely well, which was a tribute to the careful handling of Dalton and the affectionate atmosphere created by the Princess of Wales.

'Darling Motherdear' was the most important person in both their lives. They would say their prayers with her in the evening, and she taught them to reverence the Bible and to go regularly to church. When they were young she would read to them and later George read aloud to her during the daily ritual of hairbrushing. She taught them, as Queen Victoria admitted, to have 'great simplicity and an absence of all pride'.

Their grandmother was always a presence in their lives though they did not see a great deal of her. She sent them presents and a lot of good advice. On George's eighth birthday she gave him a watch 'hoping it will serve to remind you to be very punctual in everything and very exact in your duties'. In April 1876 he wrote to her describing his Easter:

Please thank Aunt Beatrice very much for that nice chocolate egg she sent me yesterday. Mama gave us some very pretty Easter eggs with lots of nice little things inside them, and ones which we had to find to the sound of music played loud when we were near and soft when we were far off. We went this morning to the farm to see some Brahmin cows which dear Papa sent home from India and we fed them with biscuits and then we went to the dairy and saw some little pats of butter made.

For Eddy and George the idyllic, indulgent period of their childhood was nearly at an end. Prince George, as the second son, was destined for the Navy and in 1877, at the age of twelve, it was time for him to enter the training ship *Britannia*. The problem was what to do with Eddy. Queen Victoria had hoped he would go to Wellington College because the Prince Consort had taken an interest in the school, but Dalton was very reluctant to see the brothers separated. 'Difficult as the education of Prince Albert Victor is now, it would be doubly or trebly so if Prince George were to leave him. Prince George's lively presence is his mainstay and chief incentive to exertion; and to Prince George again, the presence of his elder brother is most wholesome as a check against that tendency to self-conceit which is apt at times to show itself in him.' He suggested that if Eddy was to share George's naval training it would encourage 'those habits of promptitude and method, of manliness and self-reliance, in which he is now somewhat deficient'.

Queen Victoria was very ready to see her grandsons educated away from home to escape 'the constant moving from place to place – the necessary excitement going on' but she was not happy to see Eddy go to the *Britannia*: 'The very rough sort of life to which boys are exposed on board ship is the very thing not calculated to make a refined and amiable Prince, who in after years (if God spares him) is to ascend the throne.' She was also concerned that a nautical education would 'engender and encourage national prejudices and make them think that their own country is superior to any other'.

In the end, however, she agreed, and in September 1877 the two boys left the pampered life of Sandringham for the rigours of the Navy. True they were accompanied by Dalton and had a cabin to themselves but nevertheless it was an enormous contrast to the life they had left behind. For their mother too it was a dreadful wrench. She wrote to them: 'I hate to go past your dear little rooms where I have so often tucked up my dear boys for the night. Have you got to like your hammocks now and do you sleep well?' She asked Dalton to make sure that they would be 'kind to everybody, high and low, and not get grand now they are by themselves'. Thrown in suddenly among two hundred unknown boys there was little chance of their putting on airs for, as George recalled later, it never did him any good to be a Prince.

It was a pretty tough place and, so far from making any allowances for our disadvantages, the other boys made a point of taking it out on us on the grounds that they'd never be able to do it later on. There was a lot of fighting among the cadets and the rule was that if challenged you had to accept. So they used to make me go up and challenge the bigger boys – I was awfully small then – and I'd get a hiding time and time again.

Then we had a sort of tuck-shop on land . . . only we weren't allowed to bring any eatables into the ship, and they used to search you as you came aboard. Well, the big boys used to fag me to bring them back a whole lot of stuff – and I was always found out and got into trouble in addition to having the stuff confiscated. And the worst of it was, it was always *my* money; they never paid me back – I suppose they thought there was plenty more where that came from, but in point of fact we were only given a shilling a week pocket money, so it meant a lot to me, I can tell you.

But despite such problems common to all schoolboys, Prince George survived and showed particular aptitude for maths and boat sailing. Eddy on the other hand was so far behind the other cadets that the Navy hopefully suggested his parents might remove him. Alexandra would not hear of it: 'Nothing could be worse for him in every way than to be *educated at home alone* this time without even his brother!' But when the boys had served their full time in *Britannia* the problem of what to do with Eddy loomed as large as ever. The same solution was found as before; he should stay with Prince George when he joined his first ship in 1879.

The idea of sending both princes on to the high seas in the same boat caused a lot of anxiety in many quarters, and the Queen's private secretary, Sir Henry Ponsonby, has left an entertaining memorandum of the confusion that ensued.

1 Plan proposed to the Queen who did not at all like it.

2 Dalton sent by the Prince of Wales to urge it. Queen's objections not pressed.

3 Unanimous condemnation by the Cabinet of the plan.

4 Indignation of the Queen and Prince at their interference.

5 Cabinet say they didn't. Plan adopted.

6 Controversies on the selection of officers. The Queen supporting what she believed to be the Prince of Wales' choice. Sometimes it appeared he wished for others. Final agreement on the officers.

7 The *Bacchante* announced to be the ship. Who chose her, when and where I don't know.

8 Chorus of approbation.

9 Strong whispers against her. No stability. The Queen doubtful. The Prince of Wales doubtful. Dalton very doubtful – prefers *Newcastle*.

10 Smith [First Lord] furious, outwardly calm. Offers to turn over crew to *Newcastle* – an old ship full of bilge water. Sends report in favour of *Bacchante*.

11 Scott ordered to cruise in search of a storm so as to see if she will capsize.

Prince Eddy and Prince George aboard the training ship *Britannia* in December 1877. Despite the difference in their position and abilities, they remained always the best of friends.

12 Scott returns, says she won't. Dalton not satisfied. Wants to separate Princes.

13 Queen says this is what she first thought of but Dalton said it was impossible. Let him consult Prince and Princess of Wales.

14 Queen mentions doubts to Lord Beaconsfield.

15 B. observes he has already been snubbed – but if his advice is wanted, he will give it.

16 Knollys says that Dalton is wrong.

Eventually both Princes set sail in the *Bacchante* for a seven-month cruise to the West Indies. Prince George was to be treated as any other midshipman 'with the exception of keeping Night Watch, from which he is to be excused under medical advice, as well as employment on boat service in tempestuous weather'. Eddy, since he was not destined for the Navy, spent more time pursuing his studies with Mr Dalton. The only unfortunate incident of the cruise was when a journalist falsely reported that they had been tattooed on the nose while at Barbados. The Queen despatched angry telegrams but Princess Alexandra wrote in lighter vein to Prince George: 'How could you have your impudent snout tattooed.' Mr Dalton hastened to assure his employers that there was no truth in the story: 'The Princes' noses are without any fleck, mark, scratch or spot of any kind whatever.'

Prince George had passed his midshipman's exam with success and though Eddy was still lagging far behind Mr Dalton thought a longer cruise would be valuable to them both. Devoted though their mother was to her sons, she was much less selfishly possessive of them than of her daughters, and she agreed that both should make a two-year world cruise in the *Bacchante*. Prince George was only fifteen and felt the parting badly. He wrote a forlorn letter to his mother after they had made their farewells, and ended: '*So goodbye once more my darling Motherdear*, please give darling Papa and sisters my very best love and kisses.'

In their long voyage they visited Cape Town, Australia, Japan, Hong Kong, Shanghai, Singapore, Colombo, Egypt, the Holy Land and Greece. Though troubled often by seasickness Prince George worked hard, kept up his diary, read Dickens, and endured cheerfully the monotony of long weeks at sea. Commander Hillyard, a fellow sailor, described him as: 'Unselfish, kindly, good-tempered, he was an ideal shipmate.' The Commander also pointed out that though Prince George was only fourteen when he first went to sea he had 'when in charge of one of the ship's cutters for instance, to accept full responsibility for the lives of men. He also had to endure all the discomforts and all the hardships which were the inevitable and common lot of anyone who went to sea in those days.' There is no doubt that naval discipline had a profound effect on moulding Prince George's strong and dutiful character, but it is surprising that with this wonderful chance to see the world he did not get more cosmopolitan in his outlook. He had met the King of the Zulus, and the Mikado, journeyed up the Nile and toured the Holy Land, and yet the two Princes who stepped ashore at Cowes in August 1882 were still, to quote Queen Victoria 'exclusively English'.

The end of the *Bacchante*'s cruise was the end of childhood for Eddy and George. Now for the first time their paths were to diverge: Eddy was to go to Cambridge to be the despair of a new set of tutors and George was to continue his naval career. The last thing they did together was to be confirmed by Archbishop Tait at Whippingham Church soon after they landed. 'God grant that you, Sirs,' he said, 'may show to the world what Christian Princes ought to be. A great field lies before you.'

Quite what field Prince Albert Victor would shine in was perplexing all his family. Lady Geraldine Sullivan, an acquaintance of the royal family, recorded that he was 'as nice a youth as could be, simple, unaffected, unspoiled, affectionate, but! his *ignorance*! Lamentable. What on earth stupid Dalton has been about all these years! He has taught him nothing!' She also commented on his 'sleepy apathetic laziness and total want of initiative' and deplored his lack of interest even in sport. Queen Victoria was always very understanding about Eddy's backwardness – far more so than she had been with her own eldest son – and before he went to Cambridge she summoned him to Balmoral to receive the Garter and lots of good advice. Both the Queen and the Princess of Wales had great difficulty in trying to prevent the boys following in their father's footsteps without actually showing any disapproval of Bertie's way of life. After Eddy's visit to Balmoral she wrote thanking the Queen for her good advice to him and adding: 'I am particularly glad you did not allude to any of the other subjects you intended speaking about, such as races, clubs, etc. as he really has no inclination that way and it might only have put them into his head beside placing his father in an awkward position.' Sadly it turned out that dissipation was the only area in which Eddy did show any enthusiasm or aptitude.

George, on the other hand, remained dependable, cheerful and affectionate, any mother's delight. His father too was coming to take a pride in him, and as he reached manhood George's awe of his father changed into a firm friendship, which was particularly remarkable considering how different their characters were and how George must have disapproved of his father's neglect of his adored mother. As the eighteen-year-old Prince prepared to board HMS *Canada* the Princess wrote him one of her most loving letters:

I have only just left you going to bed, after having given you my last kiss and having heard you say your prayers. I need hardly say what I feel – and what we both feel at this sad hour of parting – It will be harder for you this time to have to go quite by yourself – without Eddy, Mr Dalton or Fuller – but remember darling that when all the others are far away God is always there – and He will never forsake you – but bring you safe back to all of us who love you so –

I need hardly say my darling little Georgie *how* much I shall always miss you – now we have been so much together and you were such a dear little boy not at all spoilt and so nice and affectionate to old Motherdear – Remain just as you are.

4

Sailor Princes

EDWARD

ALBERT

MARY

HENRY

GEORGE

JOHN

And wedding-bells were clamorous all the morn
With messages to men;
For lo! to England's Crown a child is born,
A bud of hope, a rose without a thorn,
A little life whose emblem is a dove,
New-sped from Heaven above,
To be acclaimed now by lute and pen.

Ode on the birth of Edward VIII,
Eric Mackay, 1894

WHEN Prince George set sail with HMS *Canada* in 1883 his only thought was to enjoy a successful career in the Royal Navy. He would have been astonished, and distressed, to know that in less than a decade the Navy would be behind him and the throne of England his inevitable, though distant, fate. For in January 1891 his elder brother Prince Eddy succumbed to pneumonia and died at Sandringham in the arms of his broken-hearted mother.

Eddy had been an anxiety to his parents ever since his birth and in the nine years since he had left the *Bacchante* they had looked in vain for any strengthening of his character and abilities. Nevertheless it was no comfort to the bereaved parents to realise that their second son was far more fitted for kingship than the eldest could have ever been. Indeed his death

71

seemed all the more tragic because his recent betrothal to Princess Mary of Teck, known to her family and the public as Princess May, had brought strong hope that Eddy would reform his ways. Just as she had arranged an early marriage for her own problem son, Queen Victoria hoped a strong-minded, sensible princess would make something of her grandson. Among the eligible young women of royal descent Princess May was a strong candidate. She was a great-granddaughter of George III through her mother, Princess Mary Adelaide, the Queen's first cousin. She was not a 'Royal Highness', however, because her mother had married a 'Serene Highness', the Prince of Teck, whose father had forfeited his rights to the throne of Württemberg because he had made a morganatic marriage. But Queen Victoria thought the prejudice of continental royal families against morganatic blood was absurd and Princess May's stalwart character and English upbringing far outweighed any disadvantages of birth. She was intelligent, attractive, dutiful, discreet and, in a word, good. Whether she could have reformed Prince Eddy is one of history's 'might-have-beens' but we can be sure she would have had a very good try. She can hardly have been in love with so feckless a youth and yet the tragedy of a young life cut short, the sorrow of his family, and the loss of her own golden prospects must have combined to make Eddy's death a traumatic experience.

Princess May was immensely popular, both for her own qualities and for her Englishness, and Eddy had scarcely been laid to rest before it was suggested that May should marry Prince George. She was so well suited to be one day a Queen Consort that the nation, from Queen Victoria downwards, saw an essential rightness in her marrying the new heir presumptive. Prince George had hoped to marry his cousin Marie of Edinburgh but she declined him, astonishingly, in favour of the Prince of Romania. In April 1893 Prince George, now Duke of York, dutifully proposed to Princess May and she dutifully accepted him.

Though they married for duty they were rewarded with a deep and lasting attachment. 'I adore you sweet May,' wrote Prince George a few months after the wedding, and seventeen years later his feelings were the same: 'My love grows stronger for you every day mixed with admiration and I thank God every day that he has given me such a darling devoted wife as you are.' Although Princess May regretted her husband's lack of intellectual or aesthetic interests, she loved and respected him and rejoiced in the fact that he needed her, for she revered the monarchy and was most anxious to play a worthy part in it.

They were married in July 1893 and in the summer of the following year the royal family waited expectantly for news from White Lodge in Richmond Park where Princess May was preparing for her first confinement. 'Dear May keeps us waiting a little, but it must be very soon,' wrote Queen Victoria in June. She admired May's maternity dress which was so well designed 'with blue lace and other very becoming arrangements that one sees very little'. This would have pleased Princess May for she shared Queen Victoria's dislike of pregnancy, both for the enforced inactivity and the attendant publicity. Vicky, now Empress of Germany, loved everything to do with babies and was disappointed to find, during May's third pregnancy, that she did not wish it remarked upon or even mentioned. A letter from Princess May to her husband echoes exactly the tone of Victoria's letters on the subject: 'Of course it is a great bore for me and requires a great deal of patience to bear it, but this is alas the penalty of being a woman.'

Her first long wait was rewarded by the birth of a son on 23 June. Prince George, who had been whiling away the anxious hours reading *Pilgrim's Progress*, wrote in his diary: 'At 10 a sweet little boy was born and weighed 8 lb. . . . Mr Asquith [Home Secretary] came to see him.' A host of telegrams despatched the news all over the world. At a ball in Windsor Great Park the Prince of Wales stopped the orchestra to propose a toast to his grandson. Equally delighted was the baby's maternal great-aunt, Augusta of Mecklenburg-Strelitz, who wrote to her sister the Duchess of Teck: 'I am still in a *twitter* can hardly take in the immense happiness of the moment! of this great Historical Event! are *you* not beside yourself? I am! and long to *squeeze* everybody who comes in my way.'

Queen Victoria was thrilled to learn of this extension to the dynasty she had founded with Albert, particularly since 'it has never happened in this Country that there shld. be 3 direct Heirs as well as the Sovereign alive'. She went to see her great-grandson when he was only four days old, accompanied by Tsarevitch Nicholas who was visiting her with his fiancée, her granddaughter 'Alicky' of Hesse.

I went over yesterday with Beatrice, Nicky, Alicky &c to see May & the Baby who is a vy fine strong Boy, a pretty Child. May I did not see, as it was rather too soon & the Doctor specially wished she shld be kept vy quiet, but she is perfectly well & Dr Williams said one could not be a stronger & healthier parent than she is – wh. is a gt. thing for the future.

It was not to be expected that the naming of such an important baby would be left to the parents. 'I am *most anxious naturally*,' wrote Queen Victoria, 'that he should bear the name of his beloved Great Grandfather, a name which brought untold blessings to the whole Empire & that *Albert* should be his 1st name.'

Prince George's reply was tactful but firm: 'Ever since I can remember I have always tried my best to be a dutiful grandson to you and never go against your wishes. Long before our dear child was born, both May and I settled that if it was a boy we should call him Edward after darling *Eddy*. *This is the dearest wish of our hearts*, dearest Grandmama, for Edward is indeed a *sacred* name to us. . . .'

In her reply Victoria voiced an old grievance: 'You write as if *Edward* was the *real* name of dear Eddy, while it was *Albert Victor*.' However, she still came to the christening and held the baby, who was dressed in the robe that had been made for Vicky over fifty years before. He was christened Edward Albert Christian George Andrew Patrick David, the last four names being the patron saints of England, Scotland, Ireland and Wales. To his family he was always David. After the service a famous photograph was taken of the four generations, the Prince of Wales and Prince George standing behind Victoria, who held the baby in her lap. The Queen was very proud of this photograph and sent signed copies to all her family and to her dominions overseas.

It may perhaps show a lack of maternalism in Princess May that six weeks after her baby's birth she left him with nurses and went with her mother on a month's holiday to St Moritz. On the other hand she may have been anxious to give her husband an excuse to recuperate at Cowes from the effects of staying with his rather overpowering mother-in-law. 'I am very fond of dear Maria,' he wrote to his wife, 'but I assure you I wouldn't go through the six weeks I spent at White Lodge again for anything.' His own mother condoled with him on being parted from 'yr sweet May & tutsoms baby' but one suspects Prince George was delighted to be back in the masculine companionship of Cowes.

To preserve her husband's sanity, Princess May gave birth to her second child, in 1895, at their own home of York Cottage, on the Sandringham estate. The Home Secretary arrived just in time for the birth and described the new prince as 'a very good-looking little man'. However, even so early in his life, the baby had committed two *faux pas*: firstly he should have been a girl and secondly he should have on no account made his entrance to the world on 14 December, the dreadful anniversary of the deaths of the Prince Consort and Princess Alice.

The royal family were anxious lest Queen Victoria took against the little one on account of his birthday and on his father's advice, Prince George swiftly wrote to the Queen proposing the name Albert:

Prince George and Princess May, Duke and Duchess of York, with their first-born, later Edward VIII, at Sandringham in 1895.

I am afraid, dear Grandmama, you were rather distressed that he was born on the 14th, that doubly sad day to you and all our family, but we hope that his having been born on that day may be the means of making it a little less sad to you. Dear Grandmama, we propose with your permission to call him *Albert*. . . .

In fact the Queen had written in her diary on hearing the news, 'I have a feeling it may be a blessing for the dear little boy and may be looked upon as a gift from God.' She expressed great pleasure to the parents that he was to be called Albert, but wrote rather grudgingly to Vicky that 'he cld hardly have been called by any other name'. However, they need certainly not have worried that she might bear the child any resentment. 'I am all impatience to see the *new* one,' she wrote to May, 'born on such a sad day but rather the more dear to me, especially as he will be called by that dear name which is the byeword for all that is great and good.'

The baby was christened at Sandringham in February. Queen Victoria, his chief godmother, was not present but she sent her gift, a bust of the Prince Consort. Little Prince Edward was there, though not yet two years old, for his parents 'thought that in years to come it would give him pleasure to know he had been present at his brother's christening'. Unfortunately when the baby began to cry Prince Edward yelled in sympathy and had to be removed. The new prince was christened Albert Frederick Arthur George. His grandmother the Duchess of Teck did not care for the name Albert and wrote prophetically: '*George* will be his *last* name and we hope some day may *supplant* the less favoured one.' And indeed, though always known to his family as Bertie, when he ascended the throne it was as George VI.

Like previous generations of royal children the two princes were handed over to the care of nurses and only saw their parents for a short time each day, but whereas Albert and Victoria, and then Princess Alexandra, had been always in and out of the nursery, Prince George and Princess May seemed quite out of touch with what went on there. They did not realise, for example, that the head nurse could hardly be bothered with little Bertie at all and would give him his afternoon bottle during a bumpy carriage ride, causing him to develop chronic stomach trouble. Prince Edward, on the other hand, she doted on, but her affection was so jealous that before bringing him down to tea with his parents, she would twist and pinch his arm. Faced with a sobbing inarticulate infant, all the parents wanted to do was send him straight back to the nursery, so there was little opportunity for an early bond to form between parents and child. In a letter to her husband Princess May talks of her first-born with all the wariness of someone dealing with an engaging but unpredictable

Prince Albert (later George VI)
photographed as a baby, at the age of
two, and at six years old.

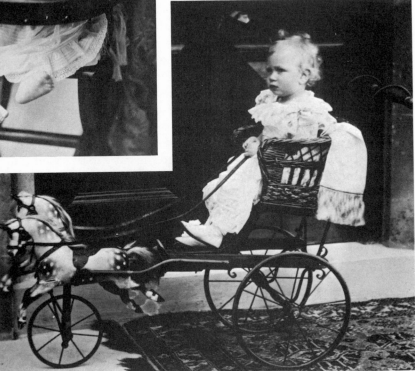

pet: 'Baby was delicious at tea this evening, he is in a charming frame of mind and I hope will be nice when you return darling tomorrow. He often calls for "Papa" and seems to miss you very much – I really believe he begins to like me at last, he is most civil to me.'

When eventually the sadistic nurse had a nervous breakdown it was discovered that she had not had a day's holiday for three years. At last Prince George and Princess May realised all was not well in the nursery and the head nurse was dismissed. She was succeeded by the kind and sensible Charlotte Bill, called 'Lala' by her charges, and greatly loved by them.

Sixteen months after the birth of Bertie, another baby was born at York Cottage and brought as much pleasure as the earlier birth had brought consternation. Not only was it a girl at last, but it was born on 25 April 1897, the year of the Jubilee. 'All happiness to you and my little Diamond Jubilee baby,' wrote Victoria. She wished the baby to be called Diamond but the Prince of Wales pointed out that no girl would want to be labelled with so clear an indication of her age. So the baby was christened Victoria Alexandra Alice Mary, and called Mary by her family.

After a three-year gap came a fourth child, Prince Henry, born on 31 March 1900. His father's cousin, Kaiser Wilhelm, was one of the godparents and wrote to Queen Victoria welcoming 'a new ray of sunshine in the pretty lodge'. Princess May rather hoped Prince Henry would be the last addition to York Cottage. In a letter to her Aunt Augusta she said,

> I confess I am just a little bit proud of myself for having another boy which was greatly wished as alas we have so few Princes in our family and now I think I have done my duty and may *stop*, as having babies is highly distasteful to me tho' when once they are there they are very nice! The children are so pleased with the baby who they think flew in at my window and had to have his wings cut off!

In fact her duty was not yet done and she was to bear two more sons, Prince George in 1902 and Prince John in 1905. 'I shall soon have a regiment, not a family,' said Prince George.

The world into which the York children were born was changing fast. Both their father and grandfather had been brought up under the eagle eye of Queen Victoria, who began to seem immortal. The supremacy of the Royal Navy, and the superiority of all things British had been taken for granted. But by the closing years of the nineteenth century the confidence of the Victorian heyday was coming to an end. The first great event of childhood that Prince Edward later recalled in his memoirs (*A King's Story*) was the outbreak of the Boer War and the shock of the early reverses

Sheik Abdullah with Prince Edward (right), Prince Albert and Princess Mary of York, 1898.

suffered by the British Army. 'In my family little else was talked about; my three Teck uncles, my mother's brothers, were all away on active service with their regiments. Their letters from the front were read aloud to us, and in the more sensational newspapers favoured by the nurses I would pore over artists' sketches of battles depicting Highlanders dying in the barbed wire in front of Magersfontein or the capture of Royal Horse Artillery guns at Colenso.' He remembered too that with the relief of Mafeking a great bonfire was lit by the Queen's highland retainers on the hill above Balmoral, just as it had been for the fall of Sebastopol in his grandfather's childhood.

A second shock to the nation's sense of security came with the death of Queen Victoria in 1901. She had been very interested in her great-grandchildren but was hurt when, as toddlers, they showed themselves to be terrified of her. 'I was a nervous child,' remembered Prince Edward, 'sensing what was in store for me, I would start to cry the moment I was led from our rooms at the Castle, and I would seldom leave off until the audience was over.' As the children grew older though, things must have improved for the Queen recorded in her diary: 'The dear little York children came, looking very well. David is a delightful child, so intellig-ent, nice and friendly. The baby [Mary] is a sweet pretty little thing.' The three elder children were taken to see the funeral service at Windsor and the interment beside the Prince Consort in the mausoleum at Frogmore. Did the young princes think ahead to the inevitable repetition of the sombre scenes on the deaths of their grandfather, father and themselves? It appears that Prince Edward at least had no such thoughts: 'At seven one's sense of destiny is limited, and one's appetite for historical pathos even more so. I remember now only the piercing cold, the interminable waits, and of feeling very lost among scenes of sorrowing grown-up relatives – solemn Princes in varied uniforms and Princesses sobbing behind heavy crepe veils.'

A few weeks later Prince George and Princess Mary sailed away in the *Ophir* for an eight-month cruise round the British Empire. David, Bertie, Mary and baby Henry were left with their delighted grandparents, now King Edward VII and Queen Alexandra. The children had a wonderful time for their grandparents were far more indulgent than their parents and liked to see children boisterous and romping. They were taken to the Military Tournament and on a fishing expedition at Virginia Water, and when they went to Sandringham for two weeks their governess Mlle Bricka was left behind in London. Affronted, Bricka complained to their distant parents who wrote protesting to Queen Alexandra. Quite unrepentant she wrote back with a splendid excuse: 'The reason we did not take her there was that Laking particularly asked that he [Edward] might be left more with his brothers and sisters *for a little while* as *we all* noticed how precocious and *old-fashioned* he was getting.'

In the autumn of 1901 the children had the excitement of sailing out in the Royal Yacht *Victoria and Albert* to meet the homing *Ophir*. King Edward had told his grandchildren that in all probability their parents had turned black during their long trip through the tropics, so it was with relief they saw two pale faces smiling down from the top of the ladder. At a family reunion at Sandringham that November Prince George was made Prince of Wales, the title which his father had borne for sixty years.

In the spring of 1902 Edward and Bertie were considered old enough to pass from the care of nurses and governess to the sterner male authority of footmen and tutors. Frederick Finch was appointed to look after the princes' physical well-being. 'In the beginning he was a sort of nanny', recollected Prince Edward, 'who shined my shoes, nursed me when I was sick, made me scrub my hands and face, and knelt beside me in the evening when I said my prayers.' Later he became a valet to the Prince and accompanied him on his travels just as Fuller had accompanied Prince George on his cruises a generation before. Finch found his charges quite a handful and was given every support from their parents when he found it necessary to spank them.

Soon after Finch was introduced into their lives, the education of the two elder Princes was entrusted to Henry Hansell, a thirty-nine-year-old bachelor schoolmaster. He was a kindly, sensible man and a keen yachtsman, which endeared him to the Prince of Wales, but he was not a great teacher. He tried to create an atmosphere of learning by fitting up a study to look as much like a classroom as possible, but he did not succeed in awakening any enthusiasm in his pupils for the pursuit of knowledge, though they did become very fond of him personally. For a short while they were joined by their younger sister but Mr Hansell found he could not cope. 'I must keep Princess Mary apart from the others as much as possible, whenever it is a matter of work,' he reported. 'Her disposition is mercurial; one can enforce discipline and order of a sort but the fact remains that, so long as she is in the room, her brothers cannot concentrate their attention on any serious work.' The Princess was therefore removed to work alone with a governess, Mlle José Dussau. Mr Hansell told the Prince of Wales that his sons would be far better off in the competitive atmosphere of a preparatory school, but the Prince would not hear of this for his elder sons.

The early years of Princess Mary and her brothers were spent chiefly at York Cottage, though they often paid visits to Marlborough House in London, Frogmore House at Windsor or Abergeldie Castle near Balmoral. York Cottage was a strangely small and unappealing home for the Prince of Wales and his family but because it was on the beloved Sandringham estate the Prince could see nothing wrong with it. His cousin Princess Alice of Athlone described it with a less partial eye:

> It was a poky and inconvenient place, architecturally repulsive and always full of the smell of cooking. George adored it, but then he had the only comfortable room in the house which was called the 'Library', though it contained very few books. The decor of this room was hideous. . . . The drawing room was small enough when only two adults occupied it – but after tea, when five children were crammed into it as well, it became a veritable bedlam.

Although the Prince of Wales wanted his children to have as happy a childhood as he had enjoyed himself, his temperament, and that of his wife, made it impossible to recreate the mutual admiration society in which he and Eddy had grown up. Where Princess Alexandra had been spontaneous and demonstrative, Princess May was shy and reserved; where Bertie had been tolerant and easy-going, Prince George was critical and unbending. He loved playing with his children when they were babies, and boasted 'I make a very good lap', but as they grew older he had no patience with the misdemeanours of childhood and no memory, it would appear, of his own rampaging youth. He wrote to his second son on his fifth birthday: 'Now that you are five years old I hope you will always try and be obedient and do at once what you are told as you will find it will come much easier to you the sooner you begin. I always tried to do this when I was your age and found it made me much happier.'

In fact of course Prince George had been a most undisciplined little boy until he went into the Navy, but he expected his children to behave from the earliest age like young naval officers. He liked, for example, to take them on walks at Sandringham but insisted on 'march discipline', and when one son appeared with hands in pockets he ordered Mrs Bill to sew up the pockets of all their sailor suits. If one of his children misbehaved in his presence a gust of wrath would descend upon the evil-doer; if he heard of it by report they were soon aware of his displeasure. 'No words that I was ever to hear', recollected Prince Edward, 'could be so disconcerting to the spirit as the summons, usually delivered by a footman, that "His Royal Highness wishes to see you in the Library".'

The Prince of Wales was a kind and generous man, greatly loved by his staff, but even when not scolding his children he found it difficult to be relaxed with them. 'His manner to them alternated between an awkward jocularity of the kind which makes a sensitive child squirm from self-consciousness, and a severity bordering on harshness,' recalled the Countess of Airlie, a lady-in-waiting. And yet he wanted to be their friend and counsellor as his father had been to him: 'I want you to treat me as your best friend,' he wrote to his eldest son. 'My great wish is that you should be happy and be fitted for the position that you will some day occupy in this country.' Sadly his sons became frightened of him instead, and remained so right up to the time they married.

Princess May had a more serene and tolerant personality than her husband and though her reserve made it difficult for her children to confide in her they had some very happy times together. Every evening as she rested before dinner the children would gather round her on little chairs and crochet comforters for one of the many charities she patronised while she read aloud to them. 'Her soft voice, her cultivated mind, the cosy room overflowing with personal treasures were all inseparable ingredients of the happiness associated with this last hour of a child's day,' remembered the Duke of Windsor. With the birth of each child she started an album recording every milestone of childhood, the first tooth, the first haircut, the first step. She did not share her husband's love for shooting, so as the children grew older there were many afternoons in which she was free to take them for picnics in Scotland, or river trips along the Thames from Windsor. She tried particularly to give them a love of history and appreciation of art which was so lacking in her husband.

Although some of her attempts to instil culture were rather above their heads she had also a sympathy for more childlike pleasures. When Prince Edward returned from Osborne one holiday she asked him what he would like to do, and when he asked for a ride in a taxi she immediately indulged him. 'A rattling contraption with a polished brass lamp and accoutrements, hard leather seats and a rubber bulb horn' was whistled up to Marlborough House and the Prince set off in it.

In understanding her sons she was hampered perhaps by the fact that the eldest three were so different from her. She had been a studious and self-controlled child, always anxious for self-improvement, and she could not understand the inattention, nervousness and lack of will to learn shown in her three elder sons. Her brains were inherited only by Princess Mary and Prince George, and it was with these two children she was most at ease. Another constraint in her dealings with her children was her reverence for her husband's position. 'I have always to remember', she told a friend, 'that their Father is also their King,' and this prevented her defending them from his wrath as much as she should have done.

However, too much should not be made of the deficiencies of Prince George and Princess May as parents. They were strict in a strict age, they had unreasonably high expectations of what their children could achieve, and they were not demonstrative, but in this they were no different to countless parents in their generation and since. Their children can never have doubted that their parents had the greatest love and concern for them and the mutual devotion of their father and mother made for a secure environment. If their faults were much rebuked, their achievements were also praised, their childish letters were immediately answered, and the smallest details of their welfare were carefully considered. If the parental regime was as oppressive as is sometimes suggested it would surely have dampened the high spirits so often commented on by observers. 'They ragged each other unmercifully,' noted a lady-in-waiting, 'and while Prince Henry and Prince George were, perhaps, even more mischievous than the others, there was not much to choose between them.' Lord Esher took the three eldest to Westminster Abbey: 'They climbed on to every tomb, and got very dirty, but were thoroughly happy.' Eight years later he visited the royal family in Scotland: 'The house is a home for children – six of them at luncheon – the youngest running round the table all the while.' One cannot imagine such informality in Victoria's day.

Like their father and grandfather the Wales children spent their early years generally isolated from their contemporaries though they did mix a little at dancing classes in London and in occasional games with the village boys in Norfolk. But like the previous generations they had the compensation of coming from a large family which provided its own companionship. In adult life Prince Edward was admired for his readiness to pick up babies, and he said it came easily to him as there had always been babies in the nursery at home. Lord Esher noted his care for his younger brothers, and their awareness of his destiny, during a visit to Windsor Castle in 1904 when David was ten and the youngest, then Prince George, was two.

I have been walked off my legs, and pulled off them by the children. The youngest is the most riotous. The eldest, a sort of head nurse. It was queer looking through a weekly paper and coming to a picture of the eldest with the label 'our future king'. Prince Albert at once drew attention to it – but the elder hastily brushed his brother's finger away and turned the page. Evidently he thought it bad taste.

Prince John, the youngest
son, who suffered from
epilepsy and died at the
age of thirteen.

Although the Wales children had long hours of lessons they did not, like Victoria's children, have to spend their leisure rehearsing French plays. The utmost asked of them was to recite verses on the occasion of their parents' birthdays, a custom which the elder children found very embarrassing, though Prince Henry would give 'The Burial of Sir John Moore' with great aplomb. Outside the classroom they were generally left free to explore all the delights of their different homes. At Windsor they would play hide and seek among the marble busts or wheel each other up and down corridors on the tall library ladder. In London at Marlborough House they loved to watch the Changing of the Guard but they were not so keen on the games of cricket on the lawn under the eagle eye of their father and Mr Hansell. One of the great excitements of the year was the train journey to Scotland in late summer. They had a 'bed-carriage' with upholstered stools to link the seats so they could lie across them. Foot-warmers were provided, covered in carpeting and filled with boiling water. Until their father became King in 1910 they went not to Balmoral but to the small grim fortress of Abergeldie. It was not the most comfort-able of royal homes but they loved it. There was the wonderful scenery all around to explore and as they grew older they were initiated into the delights of deer stalking, grouse shooting and salmon fishing.

The development of the safety bicycle at the turn of the century brought them a new freedom which they particularly enjoyed at Sandringham. 'The woodland trails of that great estate became for two boys and their sister on rubber tires an enchanted forest in which almost anything might happen, although it never did,' recalled the Duke of Windsor. The most exciting ride was down the steep hill at Wolferton station: 'Arriving at the crest, I would crouch down over the handle-bars as racing cyclists do, then pedalling as hard as I could, I would race downhill, with Mary and Bertie tearing along behind and Finch bringing up the rear, shouting hoarse warnings that I could not hear.'

Another excitement at Sandringham was the periodic arrival of King Edward and Queen Alexandra at the 'Big House', which instantly sprang into gaiety and life. When their grandchildren ran up the hill to say goodnight to the King and Queen, it was like entering a magical world, so different to the dull simplicity of York Cottage. Prince Edward in particu-lar felt far more rapport with his grandfather's life-style than with his father's: 'The Big House under his auspices seemed to me, as a child, the quintessence of all that was amusing and gay.'

As the only girl among six boys Princess Mary might have had a lonely childhood but she was so fearless on a horse or a bicycle that she easily shared in all her elder brothers' amusements. She was better at riding and games than at domestic skills – when Prince Henry tried one of her cakes on a family picnic he was heard to remark: 'I've always understood that it was high treason to speak disrespectfully of the daughter of the King.' With curly golden hair and blue eyes she was everyone's ideal of a young princess and became her father's favourite. Though he often teased her she was rarely scolded. When she was nine years old she was the only child to accompany the parents to the coronation of her Aunt Maud as Queen of Norway: 'She is as happy as the day is long at being with us here,' wrote Princess May, 'and we actually took her to the Coronation and she behaved quite beautifully thro' the long service.' She was more studious than her elder brothers; indeed Prince Edward is said to have remarked on hearing of his destiny: 'What a pity it's not Mary; she's far cleverer than I am.'

Though not especially clever at book-learning Prince Edward was an intelligent, articulate, lively and handsome boy, and a source of great pride and hope to his parents. Lord Esher wrote of him in 1906: 'Prince Edward develops every day fresh qualities, and is a most charming boy; very direct, dignified and clever. His memory is remarkable – a family tradition; but the look of Weltschmerz in his eyes I cannot trace to any ancestor of the House of Hanover.'

Sandwiched between an admired elder brother and a charming only sister, Prince Albert tended to be overshadowed and overlooked. In babyhood, as we have seen, his nurse had neglected him in favour of his elder brother, and as he grew older, though by no means neglected, he was invariably outshone. In 1907 his father wrote to a friend: 'My two eldest sons enjoyed their first day's shooting, the eldest got 12 rabbits & the 2nd got 3.' Such an unequal division of luck was the story of Bertie's life until the time of his marriage.

When he was only six Lord Esher had noted 'the second boy is the sharpest' but he soon fell behind his brother when they began lessons. This may have been partly due to a bad stammer which developed when he was seven or eight, possibly as a result of his being made to use his right hand when he was naturally left-handed. There can be few greater handicaps for a child than the frustration of being unable to express oneself, or to fight back verbally against the mockery of other children, and one can imagine what an affliction this was for a highly strung and nervous young prince. Several of his childhood characteristics reflect those of his grandfather, who had also been outshone by sister and brother and who had indeed stammered at one time; Prince Albert was disobedient, excitable, lacked concentration and experienced bouts of great anger or deep depression. And like his grandfather his frustration sometimes showed itself in violence. Mr Hansell complained in 1904, for example, that Prince Albert had caused 'two painful scenes in his bedroom' and had 'narrowly escaped giving his brother a very severe kick, it being absolutely unprovoked'. Prince Albert's German tutor reported that he was 'playful' and on being questioned more closely by the anxious father admitted: 'Your Highness, it isn't only that Prince Albert is inattentive, but when I scold him he just pulls my beard.'

His ability to concentrate in class was not helped by having to wear splints to correct his knock knees, a family disability but one which his elder brother, with customary good luck, escaped. They were painful to wear and Mr Hansell found it impossible to teach Bertie anything while he was wearing them. For a period he also had to wear the splints at night, and found them so uncomfortable that on one occasion he pleaded with Finch to be allowed to sleep without them. Moved by his tears, Finch agreed, but word was soon passed back to the Prince of Wales and Finch was summoned to the library. Drawing his trousers close around his legs the Prince exclaimed: 'Look at me. If that boy grows up to look like this, it will be your fault.' Prince Albert had to persevere and fortunately the treatment eventually proved successful.

Since the Prince of Wales was such a traditional and conservative man it is not surprising that he decided both his elder sons should follow in his footsteps and join the Navy. In 1907 Prince Edward departed for Osborne, which was no longer a royal home but had taken the place of the old *Britannia* as a training school for naval cadets. Two years later Prince Albert joined him. They had both had intensive coaching to get them through the entrance exam and they found it very hard to keep up with their classmates. After a couple of shaky terms Prince Edward managed to achieve a respectable place in the middle of the form but Prince Albert invariably occupied one of the last few places. There is no denying that it must have been very mortifying for the Prince of Wales to see his son coming in sixty-eighth out of sixty-eight and in the circumstances his letter of exhortation is a model of restraint.

You know it is Mama's and my great wish that you should go into the Navy and I believe you are anxious to do so, but unless you now put your shoulder to the wheel and really try and do your best to work hard, you will have no chance of passing any of your examinations. It will be a great bore, but if I find that you have not worked well at the end of this term, I shall have to get a master for you to work with all the holidays and you will have no fun at all. Now remember, everything

Prince George and Princess May with their complete family in 1906. From left to right: Mary, Henry (seated), baby John, George, Edward and Albert.

Prince Edward wearing the insignia of the Garter after his investiture as a Knight at Windsor, 1911.

rests with you, and you are quite intelligent and can do very well if you like.

Difficulties in the classroom shrank to insignificance compared with the major task of learning to live with other boys in a particularly spartan and disciplined atmosphere. No tutor or valet accompanied this generation of princes into the Navy. 'From the comfortable rooms of our different homes', recalled Prince Edward, 'I found myself thrust, in company with some thirty other boys, into a long, bare dormitory. The orbit of my living shrank to a hard, iron bed and a black-and-white sea chest with three compartments in which to keep my clothes, a tray and a private till.' They suffered all the usual problems of new boys at school, and quite a few extra trials because of their royal birth, but they survived to graduate to the slightly freer life of Dartmouth College.

In 1910 while Edward was at Dartmouth and Bertie still at Osborne they suffered a severe personal blow in the death of Edward vii, who had been such an indulgent grandfather to them both. Nine kings rode in the funeral cortege and behind them came two future kings of England, in their mother's coach. When the coffin arrived at Windsor Edward and Bertie marched behind their father in the slow, sad procession up to the Castle.

A year later they were taking part in the more joyous procession of their father's coronation. Edward, Albert, Mary, Henry and George all rode together in a coach to the Abbey, leaving at Buckingham Palace only the six-year-old Prince John. Prince Edward had a bigger role to play than in his grandfather's coronation for he was now Prince of Wales and had to take an oath of allegiance to his father: 'When my father kissed my cheeks, his emotion was great, as was mine.'

A worse ordeal was ahead for the new Prince of Wales; the prime minister Lloyd George decided it would be good for public relations if the ceremony of investiture, which had lapsed centuries before, were to be revived. The Prince was quite willing to learn to say in Welsh 'All Wales is a sea of song' but he objected strongly to a theatrical costume of white satin breeches and a purple velvet cloak. 'There was a family blow-up that night,' he recalled, 'but in the end my mother, as always, smoothed things over.' He endured his costume, pronounced his Welsh sentences and, though half-fainting in the heat, acquitted himself admirably. However, and here he differed from both his grandfather and his great-nephew, he did not enjoy the pomp and circumstance of being Prince of Wales. He was pleased to sink back into insignificance for his midshipman voyage in the Navy and disappointed on his return to learn that a career in the Royal Navy was considered too narrow an experience for a future king. Instead he was sent abroad, to improve his languages, and then to Oxford and then, even as the war clouds were gathering, into the army. He was twenty in 1914 and grew up just in time to enjoy a thrilling London season before hostilities opened on 4 August. 'It was a never to be forgotten sight', recorded King George v, 'when May and I with David went on to the balcony, the cheering was terrific. Please God it may soon be over and that he will protect dear Bertie's life.'

Prince Albert, as the second son, had been left to pursue his naval career and on the outbreak of war was an eighteen-year-old midshipman on HMS *Collingwood*. Ill-health interrupted his war service but he did have the excitement of taking part in the battle of Jutland. Sadly he had eventually to recognise that he was never going to be fit enough for a permanent career in the Navy, and finished his war service in the Royal Air Force.

Princess Mary was also growing up and though because of the war she missed the gaiety of a proper 'coming out' she flung herself whole-heartedly into war work, joining the VAD (Voluntary Aid Detachment) and working at Great Ormond Street until 1920.

Prince Henry's poor health as a young boy had saved him from the fate of being sent to Osborne, as his father recognised that he did not have the stamina for naval life. Instead he became the first son of a sovereign to go to school – St Peter's Court in Broadstairs. He went first as a day boy to see how he would fare: 'Write and tell me if you are pleased with the idea of the school,' asked his father. Prince Henry decided he did like it and from June 1910 he became a boarder. There were problems such as were to beset later generations of royal children: journalists and photographers took too much interest in him, and the boys found it difficult to treat him as one of themselves. However, despite the additional handicaps of splints and special boots, he did settle down and even carried off a prize for arithmetic, though lagging behind in other subjects. In 1912 he was joined by Prince George, whose charm and academic ability made school life easy for him.

In the autumn of 1913 Prince Henry moved on to Eton, where he was spared the study of Latin verses because his father, now the King, insisted his time would be better spent on French and German. He was at Eton throughout the First World War and under the constant exhortation of his parents passed into Sandhurst in 1918 to begin his army career. Prince George did not follow him to Eton, but followed his elder brothers into the Navy, going to Osborne in 1916 and passing out of Dartmouth in 1920.

Still in Norfolk when the war ended was the youngest son Prince John, who had been a great worry to his parents from a very early age when he developed epilepsy. He was an amusing child whose sayings were treasured by the family. On one occasion when his father returned from shooting at Balmoral and exchanged kisses with his wife, Prince John remarked to himself, 'She kissed Papa, *ugly* old man.' The maternal Queen Alexandra loved to baby this 'dear and precious little boy' and he was often invited to Sandringham to play with her. As he grew older his epilepsy grew worse and in 1917 it was decided he should live separately from the family. 'The time came when we dare not let him be with his brother and sister', recalled his nurse Mrs Bill, 'because it upset them so much. With the attacks getting so bad and coming so often, what else could we do?' So Prince John was moved to a farm on the Sandringham estate in the devoted care of Mrs Bill. In 1919 he died after one of his attacks, aged only thirteen. His parents were sad but resigned. Queen Mary wrote to a friend: 'For him it is a great release as his malady was becoming worse as he grew older, and he has thus been spared much suffering. I cannot say how grateful we feel to God for having taken him in such a peaceful way, he just slept quietly into his heavenly home, no pain, no struggle, just peace for the poor little troubled spirit which had been a great anxiety to us for many years, ever since he was four years old.' Queen Alexandra was heart-broken, and her thoughts went back to her own youngest son: 'Now our two darling Johnnies lie side by side.'

With his four surviving sons grown up and working hard in their different spheres, it might be hoped that their relationship with their father would have moved on to an easier footing. But unfortunately he still found nearly as much to criticise as when they were children. He had not the slightest sympathy for post-war ideas or entertainments and greatly disapproved when his sons deviated in any way from what was done when he was a young man. He remarked sadly to a friend: 'I am devoted to children and good with them. But they grow up, and you can only watch them going their own way and can do nothing to stop them. Nowadays young people don't seem to care what they do or what people think.'

But comfort was in store for him. In 1923 Prince Albert married Lady Elizabeth Bowes-Lyon and their little daughter Elizabeth was to be the joy of King George's declining years.

5

The Little Princesses

E<small>LIZABETH</small>

M<small>ARGARET</small>

Then turning from the countryside
For joy my spirit wept,
As I remembered England's pride
That in a city slept.

Two folded roses, hush'd and still,
Buds of a royal Spring,
Whose promise may the Lord fulfil
With splendid blossoming.

From *The Princesses*
by Christopher Hassall

W<small>HEN</small> Prince Albert, now Duke of York, began paying court to Lady Elizabeth Bowes-Lyon his family were afraid he was doomed to disappointment: 'You'll be a lucky fellow if she accepts you,' warned King George. For though Prince Albert was young, slim and good-looking, his shyness and his stammer had not improved over the years, and his royal birth was an even greater handicap. Lady Elizabeth was the ninth of ten children born to the Earl and Countess of Strathmore, and having grown up in a happy, carefree, affectionate family she had no wish to be suffocated in the dignity and etiquette of royal life. Charming, gay and lovely, she had no shortage of suitors, and when the Prince first proposed to her in 1921 she gently refused him.

Everybody thought the matter closed – except the Duke of York, who showed an unexpected tenacity of purpose. Perhaps he had never wanted anything else quite so much. He pursued Lady Elizabeth in London and in Scotland and gradually wore away her doubts through the strength of his own attachment. She found too that they had much in common for they shared the same upright moral values and both loved family life, country pleasures, and evenings of music and dancing. In January 1923 Prince Albert was at last able to telegraph to his parents 'All right. Bertie', and to his old friend Lady Airlie he wrote: 'It seems so marvellous to me to know that my darling Elizabeth will one day be my wife.'

He was the first of the four brothers to be married and he basked in his parents' pleasure and approval. 'The better I know and the more I see of your dear little wife,' the King wrote to him shortly after the wedding, 'the more charming I think she is and everyone fell in love with her here.' Free from the constraints of living with his parents, Prince Albert blossomed in the atmosphere of love, sympathy and understanding created by his wife. His luck had turned at last.

Their first home was White Lodge in Richmond Park but they soon found it had neither the convenience of a town house nor the privacy of a country retreat. While they looked for a home in London they stayed with the Duchess's parents in Bruton Street, W1, and it was there, three years after their wedding, that the Duchess gave birth to a baby girl on 21 April 1926. It was a difficult labour and eventually a Caesarian operation had to be carried out.

The King and Queen were woken in the early morning with the news and later that day they went to visit their first granddaughter. (They already had a grandson, born to Princess Mary and Viscount Lascelles earlier that year.) The Queen found 'a little darling with a lovely complexion and fair hair', but said to the baby: 'I wish you were more like your little mother.' As the *Daily Mail* pointed out, 'The baby who was the chief topic of conversation throughout the kingdom yesterday could conceivably become Queen of England,' but most of the papers stressed that the princess was third in line of succession 'for the time being'. Everyone assumed that the baby's uncle, the Prince of Wales, would soon marry and have children.

In a letter to his mother Prince Albert poured out his delight in becoming a father:

You don't know what a tremendous joy it is to Elizabeth and me to have our little girl. We always wanted a child to make our happiness complete, and now that it has at last happened, it seems so wonderful and strange. I am so proud of Elizabeth at this moment after all that she has gone through during the last few days, and I am so thankful that everything has happened as it should and so successfully. I do hope that you and Papa are as delighted as we are, to have a

The Duchess of York with Princess Elizabeth. The baby is wearing the coral necklace which the Duchess had been given as a child.

granddaughter, or would you have sooner had another grandson? I know Elizabeth wanted a daughter. May I say I hope you won't spoil her when she gets a bit older.

The Duke and Duchess of York wanted to call their daughter Elizabeth Alexandra Mary, and to their relief the King agreed. Was the baby simply named after her mother or did her parents bear in mind that Elizabeth was also the name of England's greatest Queen? In his letter to the King, Prince Albert simply said: 'It is such a nice name and there has been no one of that name in your family for a long time.' The King noticed that there was no suggestion of including Victoria but decided this was not necessary. When she grew up the Princess may have been sorry for this omission, as she was to have a high regard for Victoria's achievements. In the family she was called 'Lilibet'.

The Duchess of York breast-fed her baby for the first month, then, having to resume official life, handed her into the loving arms of Mrs Clara Knight, called 'Alah' by her charges, who had been her own nanny twenty-five years before. At five weeks the baby was christened in the private chapel at Buckingham Palace, with Jordan water from the gold lily font made for the christening of Vicky, Princess Royal, in 1840. 'Of course poor baby cried,' wrote Queen Mary afterwards.

In August 1926 the baby made the first of many journeys north to her mother's ancestral home, Glamis Castle, where she was warmly welcomed by her grandparents, Lord and Lady Strathmore, and by the devoted retainers who remembered her mother as a little girl. None of the many ghosts of Glamis haunted the baby as she slept among the yew trees in the Dutch garden just below her nursery.

Back in London in the autumn the Duchess of York had to face up to the first of many conflicts between duty and natural feeling, the prospect of which had made her so wary of a royal marriage. The King had decided that in the New Year of 1927 the Yorks should embark on an extended tour of the Antipodes, which would separate them from their baby for six long months. In between fittings for clothes and trips with her husband to a speech therapist, the Duchess spent as many hours as possible with Princess Elizabeth. A friend visiting the Duchess at this time found the Princess 'sitting up by herself in the middle of the huge chesterfield, like a white fluff of thistledown. The baby is always good, she has the sweetest air of complete serenity.'

The baby's first Christmas at Sandringham was overshadowed by the approaching separation. The Duchess's parting present was a necklace of coral beads which she had worn herself as a child. On 6 January the King and Queen and the baby said goodbye to the travellers at Victoria Station. 'I felt very much leaving on Thursday,' the Duchess later wrote to Queen Mary, 'and the baby was so sweet playing with the buttons on Bertie's uniform that it quite broke me up.'

With both sets of grandparents eager to look after the little girl, her time was tactfully divided between them. She went first to the Bowes-Lyon's English home at St Paul's Walden Bury in Hertfordshire, where two good-natured chows allowed her to grab at their fur, and then to her royal grandparents at Buckingham Palace. Every day Alah brought her down at teatime to see them – 'Here comes the bambino,' Queen Mary would exclaim. The King was already in thrall to his little granddaughter and sent detailed reports to his son on her progress: 'Your sweet little daughter . . . is growing daily,' he wrote in March. 'She has four teeth now, which is quite good at eleven months old, she is very happy.' Photographs were taken every few weeks to send to the Duke and Duchess of York, who were most anxious to watch their baby's development, even at a distance.

At last on 27 June they arrived back in London after a most successful tour, and drove through cheering crowds to be reunited with Princess Elizabeth at Buckingham Palace. When the crowd called for the royal family to appear on the balcony, the baby came out too, held in Queen Mary's arms beneath a large umbrella. The Yorks now had a London home of their own to return to, 145 Piccadilly, and here again they had to appear on the parapet to acknowledge the welcome of the crowd below. Only then could they retire into privacy and a real reunion with their baby daughter.

During their tour the Duke and Duchess had been amazed at the interest shown in their daughter. By the end they had amassed three tons of presents for her, and an immense cabinet in her day nursery was soon overflowing with china cottages, filigree furniture, little glass birds and animals, and hundreds of other knicknacks from all over the Empire. With each year of the Princess's life public affection for her seemed to increase. By the time she was six she had appeared on the cover of *Time* magazine and on the stamps of Newfoundland, she was featured on her pony among the waxworks at Madam Tussaud, her portrait had hung at the Royal Academy, and a territory in the Antarctic had been named Princess Elizabeth Land. The Duchess of York, who only wanted for her daughter the simple uncomplicated childhood that she had known, was not altogether happy at the amount of attention focused on the little Princess. 'It almost frightens me that the people should love her so much,' she wrote to Queen Mary in 1929. 'I suppose that it is a good thing, and I hope that she will be worthy of it, poor little darling.'

The chief of the Princess's admirers remained King George v. 'He was fond of his two grandsons, Princess Mary's sons,' remembered the Countess of Airlie, 'but Lilibet always came first in his affections. He used to play with her – a thing I never saw him do with his own children – and loved to have her with him.' Indeed the old King enjoyed her company so much that when he was convalescing at Bognor after a serious illness in 1929 the presence of the Princess was prescribed by his doctors. Residents of Bognor were charmed by the sight of the prattling little girl running beside the King's bathchair. Princess Elizabeth was quite unafraid of the King, despite his hot temper and booming voice. The Archbishop of Canterbury arrived one day to find his revered monarch on hands and knees, with the Princess pulling him along by his beard. On another occasion when they had a minor disagreement and the King marched out in a huff, the Princess called him back and told him off for not closing the door. King George must have been very touched when one Christmas, hearing the carol singers proclaiming joy 'to you and all mankind', the Princess exclaimed: 'I know that old man kind. That's you Grandpapa England. You are old, and you are very, very kind.'

In the summer of 1930 Princess Elizabeth was with her parents at Glamis, where the Duchess of York was awaiting the birth of a second child. The Home Secretary, John Clynes, had a long wait but at last on 21 August he was summoned to view the new baby. 'I found crowded round the baby's cot the Duke of York, Lord and Lady Strathmore and Lady Rose Leveson-Gower, the duchess's sister. They at once made way for me, and I went to the cot and peeping in I saw a fine chubby-faced little girl lying wide awake. It seemed to me that everybody was happy.'

Perhaps Mr Clynes thought it necessary to stress the happiness of all concerned because it was no secret that the parents had hoped for a boy. In the four years since the arrival of Princess Elizabeth, 'Uncle David', the Prince of Wales, had shown no sign of settling down with a wife and family, and though no one foresaw the Abdication, it did begin to seem possible that he might remain unmarried and the throne pass eventually to the Duke of York. The birth of the Duke's second child was therefore awaited with some interest and, with males predominating on both sides of the family, everyone had expected a boy. So strong was this expectation that no girls' names had been considered, and when the Duchess did eventually choose Ann Margaret, it was only to have the first name vetoed by the King. More debate followed before Margaret Rose was finally chosen and approved. It was not till October that the Duke of York went to register the names at the village store in Glamis, and meanwhile parents all over the country had registered their daughters by surname only until the royal names were announced.

Public interest in the new arrival was fully gratified by Sir Henry Simpson, the doctor who had delivered her. He offered 'some particulars about the Royal baby which will be of interest to mothers everywhere'. Her eyes were vivid blue, her hair between light and medium brown, and the shape of her lips showed a marked resemblance to her mother's. 'She is a remarkably contented baby', Sir Henry continued, 'but when she does cry she gives ample proof of her possession of lusty lungs.' Despite the disappointment over her sex Princess Margaret was warmly welcomed as the first royal baby to be born in Scotland since Charles I. A great beacon was lit on the hills above Glamis in celebration of the event and when she was christened at Buckingham Palace an enormous cake was sent down from Scotland, most of which then returned to be divided among the Glamis tenants and servants.

The birth of Princess Margaret ushered in five very peaceful years for the Duke and Duchess of York. Although they maintained a round of official duties and functions they had plenty of time to enjoy bringing up their children in their two homes, 145 Piccadilly and Royal Lodge, Windsor. The Royal Lodge was given to them by the King in 1931 and though it required an immense amount of restoration and improvement, their combined skill at home-making gradually turned it into the most gracious and welcoming of family houses.

It was to the Royal Lodge that an apprehensive young Scotswoman, Marion Crawford, came in 1932 to be governess to Princess Elizabeth, then rising six. Miss Crawford had trained as a teacher in Edinburgh and intended to make her life's work among deprived children, but before settling down to her vocation she took a temporary job teaching the children of two families near her home at Dunfermline. One of her employers was Lady Rose Leveson-Gower, sister to the Duchess of York, and through Lady Rose the Duke and Duchess came to hear of this energetic young governess, who enjoyed walking several miles every day between her two families. Miss Crawford was astonished when one day Lady Rose told her she was to be invited to undertake the education of the two Princesses. 'The Duke, I gathered, had throughout his own childhood been hampered by somewhat immobile pastors and masters. He wanted someone energetic with his children, and had been impressed with the amount of walking I did!'

Marion Crawford was very doubtful as to how well she would fit into the ducal household and how she could possibly cope with the young Princesses. 'It was a couple of very spoiled and difficult people I somehow visualised as I travelled south, for already the papers had produced odd stories about these Royal children. I was more than convinced that my month's trial would stop at the end of the month, and that I should soon be home again.' In fact 'Crawfie' was to become a most valued friend and counsellor to the whole family and stayed with them for sixteen years. When she finally left the royal service in the late 1940s she wrote her memoirs in a book entitled *The Little Princesses*. The royal family apparently regarded this as a betrayal of trust, but for the reader it is an intimate, affectionate and often amusing account of royal childhood, and will be much quoted in this chapter.

Crawfie had charge of Princess Elizabeth from nine to six each day but her out-of-school life remained in the care of Alah and the under-nurse Margaret McDonald, nicknamed Bobo, who shared a bedroom with the Princess throughout her childhood. Bobo's sister Ruby had joined the nursery after Princess Margaret was born and the two sisters became close friends and personal maids to the two Princesses. At the time of Crawfie's arrival Princess Margaret was only two and therefore not old enough for lessons but she was a bright and vivacious little girl and longed to join in all her elder sister's activities. Alah, however, wanted to have one baby still in the nursery and she kept Margaret penned up in a pram long after she wanted to be running about. She was so much kept back that a rumour began to circulate that there was something wrong with her. 'One school of thought had it that she was deaf and dumb,' wrote Crawfie, 'a notion not without its humour to those who knew her.'

Crawfie's task as governess proved a far more relaxed affair than for previous generations of royal tutors. 'No one ever had employers who interfered so little. I had often the feeling that the Duke and Duchess, most happy in their own married life, were not over concerned with the higher education of their daughters. They wanted most for them a really happy childhood, with lots of pleasant memories stored up against the days that might come and, later, happy marriages.'

As a result the Princesses' educational timetable was far less demanding than those of their royal ancestors. Formal lessons lasted only from 9.30 to 11 o'clock and were followed by an hour's break and another hour of quiet reading. After lunch the afternoon would be devoted to singing, drawing, dancing, piano lessons or an educational visit with Queen Mary. Like her husband, the Queen enjoyed the company of her grand-

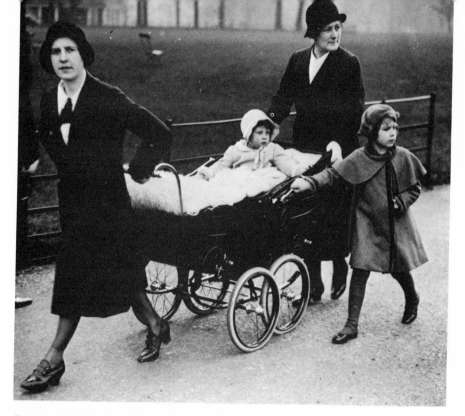

Princess Elizabeth and Princess Margaret with their nanny 'Alah' and nursemaid 'Bobo'.

Princess Elizabeth enjoyed riding from the age of four.

children more than she had that of her own children and she loved to take Elizabeth and Margaret to historic places like the Tower of London. She was also very interested in Crawfie's syllabus and suggested that for these children history and geography were more important than arithmetic. This was just as well for Princess Elizabeth never did progress very far with mathematics, though intelligent and quick to learn in other subjects.

To their parents' delight both Elizabeth and Margaret became very accomplished in the social arts befitting a princess. Singing and dancing came very easily to them and Princess Margaret proved to have a remarkable gift for music. She had astonished her grandmother Lady Strathmore by humming the Merry Widow waltz before she was a year old, and by the age of two could sing in perfect tune any song she heard. She took to piano lessons like a duck to water and by her late teens she was a very good pianist. Riding was another important skill for the Princesses to learn and fortunately they both loved horses, real or toy. Princess Elizabeth began riding at the age of four and by six had dispensed with the leading rein. Her teacher was the Duke's stud groom, Owen, who became such a hero to her that on one occasion her father remarked impatiently, 'Don't ask me, ask Owen. Who am I to make suggestions?' Owen himself was charmed by his two royal pupils: 'Words fail me to thoroughly explain how very nice Princess Elizabeth really is,' he wrote in a letter, 'and I can see Princess Margaret getting to be just as nice. I feel the proudest and most fortunate man in the world to have had the honour and the pleasure to have had the company and the teaching of these two most lovely Princesses.'

Fortunately the two sisters were not quite as perfect as this eulogy would suggest. Princess Elizabeth was basically a good, sweet-natured child, but she was capable of occasional rebellion, as when she upturned an inkwell on her head to break the tedium of a French lesson. Princess Margaret was much naughtier but with such cheeky charm that she often got away with it. When someone tried to scold her she would start singing softly 'Who's afraid of the big bad wolf'. She was not as sensitive to other people's feelings as her sister – once prodding a large visitor with the comment 'Is *all* that *you*?' – but when she chose she could be as gracious and dignified as her mother. The playwright Sir James Barrie found her most entertaining:

My most delicious memory of her is the day when she was three years old, and I had the glory of sitting beside her at her birthday tea party. Some of her presents were on the table, and they seemed to me to be simple things that might have come from the sixpenny shops, but she was in a frenzy of glee about them, especially about one which she had given the place of honour by her plate. I said to her as one astounded 'Is that really your very own?' And she saw how I envied her and immediately placed it between us with the words 'It is yours *and* mine'.

Barrie was so taken with this line that he included it in his play *The Boy David* and arranged to give Princess Margaret a penny each time it was performed.

Crawfie took to heart the Duke's anxiety that his daughters should have a lively childhood, and introduced them to grubby games of hide and seek in the bushes of Hamilton Gardens at the back of 145 Piccadilly. Many eyes watched them through the garden railings but the children were oblivious of them and soon Crawfie was too. They began to venture further afield into the space of Hyde Park but though the Princesses would gaze wistfully at the other children, 'mystic beings from another world', they were not encouraged to make friends with them. Crawfie thought this was a pity and seized every opportunity, such as dancing classes or swimming lessons, to help the Princesses mix with other children. The fact remained that they had no close friends, though there were plenty of cousins to play with, especially during their annual holiday at Glamis.

Living most of the year in the very centre of London, they were far more conscious of being cut off from the bustling world outside than they would have been at Sandringham or Windsor. They used to look out of the nursery windows at the top of the house to watch the buses rolling past and deluge Crawfie with questions about the real world beyond their home. For a while Crawfie managed to open up their lives a little with occasional forays into London. A most memorable day was their first ride on an underground train at Tottenham Court Road to have tea at the YWCA: 'Tea out of thick cups, other people's bread and butter, tea you paid for with money, these were wonderful treats.' Another jaunt was to ride on a bus, on the top deck, so that they could look down into other people's gardens. Sadly these adventures had to come to an end when the IRA began to be active in London.

The little Princesses saw much more of their parents than most children of the upper classes. 'No matter how busy the day, how early the start that had to be made, each morning began with high jinks in their parents' bedroom.' If the Duke and Duchess were at home they lunched with their daughters at midday, and they met again for tea and an hour of play before bedtime. When the little girls were in their bath their parents would join them for more fun and games, and stay until they were safely tucked into bed. On Friday afternoons the whole family drove down to the Royal Lodge for a relaxing weekend. Here the children learned to cultivate their gardens, look after their pets, and clean and tidy the Little House presented to Princess Elizabeth on her sixth birthday by the Welsh people.

The Duke and Duchess tried to keep the children's lives as simple as possible. Though much in demand they went to few parties and the even tenor of their days was disturbed only by annual treats such as a pantomime, the Military Tournament, the Horse Show or the Aldershot Tattoo. They rarely appeared on official occasions and so their participation in the King's Silver Jubilee celebrations in May 1935 was particularly memorable for them. The highlight of events was the procession through London to St Paul's Cathedral for a thanksgiving service. They made a charming picture, as Chips Channon recorded in his diary: 'The Yorks in a large landau with the two tiny pink children. The Duchess of York was charming and gracious, the baby princesses much interested in the proceedings and waving.'

As the landau left Buckingham Palace a prophetic voice had cried out, 'There goes the hope of England!', and if King George v had heard these words he would have been in complete agreement with them. Not only was his eldest son still unmarried, but this last year of the old King's life was overshadowed by the knowledge that his heir was infatuated with a woman totally unsuited to become his queen. The King's only consolation lay in the sterling qualities of his second son and his elder granddaughter: 'I pray to God', he said, 'that my eldest son will never marry and have children, and that nothing will come between Bertie and Lilibet and the throne.'

Seven months after the Jubilee the two Princesses went alone to Sandringham for Christmas. The Duchess of York was confined at Royal Lodge with influenza, and the Duke stayed with her, but they did not want to deprive the King of his granddaughters' company. It was a happy decision, for it turned out to be his last Christmas. Shortly after the little Princesses had been sent back to Royal Lodge, the old King died. Princess Margaret was too young to be much moved by events. 'Grandpapa has gone to heaven', she remarked philosophically, 'and I'm sure God is finding him very useful.' For the nine-year-old Princess Elizabeth, though, it was the loss of a true friend and counsellor, and King George remained in her memory as the model of what a constitutional monarch ought to be. She went to Windsor for the solemn service at St George's

The Princesses were usually dressed in the most sensible of clothes but for this photograph taken just before the Coronation they were allowed to look as princesses should, all frills and flounces.

The royal family in 1936 outside the little house given to Princess Elizabeth by the people of Wales.

Chapel, where, thirty-five years earlier, her father as a little boy had watched the funeral of Queen Victoria.

Life appeared to return to normal after the King's death but in fact change and speculation were in the air. In the spring of 1936 their favourite uncle, 'Uncle David', brought Mrs Simpson to meet the Duke and Duchess of York at Royal Lodge. She found the two Princesses 'so blonde, so beautifully mannered, so brightly scrubbed, that they might have stepped straight from the pages of a picture book'. The Princesses did not know of course that the new King wanted to marry this American divorcee but they did notice that he came to see them less often and had lost his natural gaiety.

By December 1936 Edward VIII had made up his mind. If he could not marry Mrs Simpson as King, he would renounce the throne in order to do so. The Duke of York was shattered by the news. That his much-admired elder brother could calmly shrug off his responsibilities was disillusioning enough, but even more appalling was the fact that he, the shy younger brother, would have to step into the breach. He had not the slightest desire to be King, nor to pass the burden on to his dearly loved daughter.

Elizabeth and Margaret, now aged ten and six, were dismayed at the news they would have to live in Buckingham Palace. 'You mean for ever?' they asked Crawfie. On 12 December the new King left home to hear his proclamation. Crawfie explained to the Princesses that from now on he was King of England. 'When the King returned, both little girls swept him a beautiful curtsey. I think perhaps nothing that had occurred had brought the change in his condition to him as clearly as this did. He stood for a moment touched and taken aback. Then he stooped and kissed them both warmly.'

In his farewell broadcast Edward VIII had said of his brother: 'He has one matchless blessing, enjoyed by so many of you and not bestowed on me – a happy home with his wife and children.' It was said to gain sympathy for himself but in fact focused public attention on the most reassuring aspect of their new King, his impeccable family life. He had always seemed so inarticulate and retiring compared with his dashing elder brother that many people viewed his succession with a distinct lack of confidence. However, the new royal family were so appealing, so good-looking, so utterly charming, that public affection and admiration quickly healed over the wound to the monarchy's reputation caused by the departure of Edward VIII. The little Princesses, of course, had long been the focus of sentimental attention; even before the abdication several books were published about them, including one, *Our Princesses and Their*

Dogs, devoted entirely to the royal canine pets. No two children, it appeared, had ever had such a wonderful relationship with their dogs as these two. And yet though they were consistently idealised their public image remained a very human one. As the *Daily Telegraph* pointed out in its coronation supplement of 1952: 'The little Lilibet was the child, not only of the Duke and Duchess of York as she pushed her doll's pram behind the traffic roar outside 145 Piccadilly; she was everybody's daughter. The eleven-year-old whose coronet tilted so entrancingly over one eye at her father's coronation was an incarnation of universal childhood.'

Preparations for the coronation and settling into Buckingham Palace absorbed the first five months of the new reign. In between fittings for their robes and coronets the two Princesses studied a thirty-foot-long panorama of George iv's coronation procession, given to them by Queen Mary, and Elizabeth read a specially bound copy of the coronation service that her father gave her. On the day itself they went with Queen Mary to Westminster Abbey, and the coach carrying the old Queen and her granddaughters was even more loudly cheered than that of the King and Queen themselves. Princess Elizabeth was anxious that her younger sister should not disgrace them all by falling asleep in the long service, but afterwards she reported to Crawfie that Margaret had behaved admirably: 'I only had to nudge her once or twice when she played with the prayer books too loudly.' Back at the Palace there were repeated balcony appearances and an hour of photography before the Princesses could get out of their finery and rest.

Much as the new King and Queen would have loved to maintain the closeness of their family life, it proved impossible amidst the interminable corridors of Buckingham Palace, and with an exacting round of new duties. The children still went to their parents' bedrooms first thing in the morning, but the King and Queen were often not in for lunch and the bed-time romp was frequently abandoned or curtailed because of evening engagements. Only when they could get away to Royal Lodge at weekends did they really relax together as a family.

After the move to Buckingham Palace King George and Queen Elizabeth grew particularly anxious that their daughters should not be too cut off from the real world. They wanted them to feel members of the community. 'Just how difficult this is to achieve, if you live in a palace, is hard to explain,' wrote Crawfie. 'A glass curtain seems to come down between you and the outer world, between the hard realities of life and those who dwell in a court, and however hard a struggle is made to avoid it, escape is not entirely possible.' It was decided it would be a good thing to form a guide company at Buckingham Palace where the Princesses could consort freely with other children. Miss Violet Synge, who was asked to captain the company, was very doubtful about its prospects. 'A guide is a friend to all and a sister to every other guide' ran one of the guide laws – how could this work at Buckingham Palace? At the first meeting her worst hopes were realised:

> The glass doors on to the terrace were flung open by scarlet-coated footmen, and down the steps came the recruits – fourteen little cousins or friends all dressed in their best, hairs beautifully curled and white gloves completing the bright array; whilst skirmishing on the sidelines were the nannies, mademoiselles and frauleins.

Her only comfort was that the two Princesses themselves were very sensibly dressed and eager to get started. Princess Margaret was too young to be a guide but Princess Elizabeth was determined she should not be left out: 'She is very strong you know. You can't say those aren't a very fine pair of hiking legs, Miss Synge. And she loves getting dirty, don't you, Margaret? And how she would love to cook sausages on sticks.' So until she grew older Princess Margaret was attached to the company as a Brownie.

Miss Synge was faced with a problem unique in her experience. Instead of trying desperately to control an unruly mob, at the Palace she had 'to incite these children to let themselves go, to run, to climb, and to do all those things that the eleven- to fourteen-year-old is usually all too willing to do'. Gradually she succeeded and the children enjoyed all sorts of guiding activities but there was always an air of unreality about the proceedings. The Princess Royal enrolled the recruits, every hike was accompanied by a detective, and sudden appearances of the King or Queen were rather unnerving for everyone. When the war came and the company was re-formed at Windsor Castle, Miss Synge's efforts to run a proper guide camp were frustrated by the helpfulness of the Windsor establishment. The Grenadier Guards put the tents up, the Home Guard provided the equipment, the Office of Works drove up with a flagpole and stores came from the head steward. Nevertheless the Windsor company did serve a useful purpose for it contained some cockney evacuees who treated the Princesses in a very casual way and made no attempt, as some of the Buckingham Palace company had, to relieve them of all the unpleasant tasks.

In the spring of 1939 the King and Queen left England for a seven week tour of North America. Queen Mary took the opportunity to pack in lots of educational visits to museums, art galleries, the Bank of England and the Royal Mint. The two Princesses were very touched by the number of letters and photos they received from Canada and the United States giving them news of their parents, and thoroughly enjoyed the bundles of comics which were sent to cheer them up. It was the first time they were made so plainly aware how many unknown people far away took a close interest in their welfare. The return of the King and Queen was a great event in their lives for they were taken out in a destroyer to meet the *Empress of Britain* in mid Channel. After a perilous transfer in a barge they stumbled eagerly up the ship's ladder to a joyful reunion.

A few weeks later came another momentous event, though it passed almost unnoticed at the time. The King was holding an inspection at the Royal Naval College at Dartmouth, where he had once been a cadet, and he took his family with him. One of the present generation of cadets was the eighteen-year-old Prince Philip of Greece, a great-great grandson of Queen Victoria, descended from her second daughter, Princess Alice. He joined the royal party to help entertain the Princesses and won their admiration with the amount he ate and his skill at jumping the tennis nets. Princess Elizabeth was thirteen and it was her first meeting with the man she was to marry eight years later.

The royal family were in Scotland when war was declared on 3 September 1939. The King and Queen hastened south, leaving Crawfie and the Princesses in the highlands until December when the family gathered at Sandringham to celebrate Christmas in the traditional royal way, which dated back to Victoria and Albert. It was a happy time but anxiety about the war cast its shadows across them. 'I kept thinking of those sailors [lost on the *Royal Oak*]', Elizabeth told Crawfie, 'and what Christmas must have been like in their homes.'

In the New Year the King and Queen went back to London to be in the centre of things, and the Princesses went to Royal Lodge, where their parents could join them at weekends. There was some talk of their being sent to Canada for safety but the Queen would not hear of it: 'The children won't leave without me, I won't leave the King, and the King will never leave.' However, as the war began to enter a more disastrous phase, in May 1940, Royal Lodge was not considered safe enough for the Princesses and they moved to Windsor Castle. Situated directly beneath the bomber routes to London, the Castle was not nearly as safe as Balmoral would have been, but the King and Queen wanted their daughters close enough for the family to be together at weekends.

A castle is not homely at the best of times but stripped of its treasures, bristling with anti-aircraft guns, enveloped in the blackout, Windsor was a grim place for the Princesses to spend the next five years. At a time when their lives and their interests should have been broadening out they were more restricted than ever, their days spent in the schoolroom and their nights in the nursery or – when there was an air-raid warning – in the gloom of the dungeons.

Crawfie did what she could to brighten up the routine. The re-formed guide company had the whole of Windsor Great Park to explore and a tame company of Grenadier Guards to fix up an assault course for them. The Guards also supplied a little social life, joining the household at lunch time and inviting the Princesses to tea in the guard room. Then to cheer the first Christmas at Windsor the Princesses and local evacuees acted a nativity play, which was so successful that their ambitions rose to a pantomime. With the help of a master and pupils from the Royal School at Windsor Great Park, they performed old favourites such as Cinderella, Aladdin, Dick Whittington and Mother Goose. Their stage was the one erected by Queen Victoria in the Waterloo Room for family theatricals of a previous generation, and the costumes and props were magnificent. Whatever else its deficiencies Windsor was not short on silks and brocades, sedan chairs or velvet curtains.

The King was thrilled to see his daughters star in the pantomimes with such aplomb. Their confidence in company never ceased to astonish him: 'I don't know how they do it,' he said to Crawfie once. 'We were always so terribly shy and self-conscious as children. These two don't seem to care.'

There was one pantomime though when Princess Elizabeth cared very much how well she acted, for Prince Philip was sitting in the front row. They began to correspond in a cousinly way and from time to time he spent his leave at Windsor Castle. Princess Elizabeth had been devoted to him since the first meeting and though she was only a child when the war began, her attachment never faltered throughout her teenage years. Prince Philip was too busy with his war service in the Royal Navy to think seriously about the future, but as the Princess grew from a sweet and lovely child to a sweet and lovely woman, his interest deepened. In 1944, when Elizabeth was eighteen, he asked his cousin King George of Greece to find out how such a match would be regarded. 'We both think she is too young for that now', replied George vi, 'as she has never met any young men of her own age. . . . P. had better not think any more about it for the present.'

With every year that had passed since the abdication it seemed more

Princess Elizabeth and Princess Margaret leaving the YWCA with their governess, Marion Crawford, in 1939. They had just had their first ride on a tube train.

Princess Elizabeth and Princess Margaret in their costumes for *Cinderella*, which they performed at Windsor Castle for Christmas 1941.

likely that Princess Elizabeth would one day become Queen and would not be supplanted by a younger brother. It was never talked about, Crawfie tells us, but it was never far from the minds of those responsible for bringing her up. Before the war she was beginning to appear more often in public – taking the salute at a march past of scouts, for example, and greeting President Lebrun of France, in fluent French. Unfortunately the war diminished such opportunities to learn the royal craft, but her studies were broadened by lessons on constitutional history with Sir Henry Marten at Eton. In October 1940, aged fourteen, she broadcast to children all over the Empire: 'I can truthfully say to you all that we children at home are full of cheerfulness and courage.' At the end she called her sister to the microphone and a little voice piped up 'Good night, children'.

Princess Elizabeth's anxiety to include her sister in everything dated from earliest childhood. Sir James Barrie had been touched years before by 'the Princess Elizabeth's pride in her little sister whenever the Princess Margaret won a game. . . . It was like the pride of a mother, though it began, to my eyes, when both were little more than babes.' Princess Elizabeth was so unsophisticated a child, and Princess Margaret such a forward one, that the four-year gap between them never diminished their companionship. The age difference was further reduced by the custom of dressing them in identical clothes, even as late as 1943, when Chips Channon noticed at a thanksgiving service 'the two Princesses dressed alike in blue, which made them seem like little girls'.

As Princess Margaret grew older her elder sister's anxiety was not only that she should not be left out but that she should behave with decorum. 'If you do see someone with a funny hat, Margaret, you must *not* point at it and laugh,' she warned her before a garden party. She was deeply embarrassed by her sister's fondness for practical jokes, and hated to see her showing off. 'Stop her, Mummie. Oh please stop her!' she would plead when Margaret was being particularly outrageous and amusing.

But the King and Queen took a great delight in their gay, mischievous, talented younger daughter, who would play, act, and sing with equal skill, and keep them in fits of laughter with her brilliant mimicry. Recognising perhaps that she needed to compensate for being the youngest, they indulged her antics and gave her much more freedom than her elder sister.

Nevertheless Princess Margaret was always impatient with the cage of royalty which surrounded her. As Crawfie said, 'She fretted at the restrictions which so often prevented her from learning about life and

Princess Elizabeth makes her first broadcast in October 1940. At the end she called her sister to the microphone to say goodnight.

As Girl Guide patrol leaders in 1943 the Princesses practise with pigeon post.

people at first hand. "I want to *know* about people, Crawfie" she would say in an almost despairing voice.' When evacuees were co-opted into the guide company Princess Margaret was always attracted to the most cockney ones, and at camp, while her elder sister made excuses to sleep in privacy in the summer house, Margaret adored being thrust into a tent with half a dozen others. Her patrol was always the most riotous, Crawfie noticed:

Every evening I would watch the same performance. From the tent that housed Margaret there would burst forth storms of giggles. The Guides officer would appear, say a few well chosen words, and retreat. The ensuing silence would reign for a minute or two, then a fresh outburst probably meant Margaret was giving her companions an imitation of the Guides officer's lecture.

It was strange that with both George V and George VI having been younger brothers, no thought was given to Princess Margaret's chances of succeeding; there were no lessons in constitutional history for her. She was a great joy and diversion to her parents, but the serious, sweet-natured Princess Elizabeth was their pride. The King in particular would confide in her as in an equal and as she grew older he took the greatest trouble to initiate her into her future role. When she was sixteen he made her a colonel of the Grenadier Guards and she took her duties so earnestly that after one inspection Crawfie was asked to 'tell the Princess quietly that the first requisite of a really good officer is to be able to temper justice with mercy'. She longed to do war work and after much persuasion her father allowed her to join the ATS (Auxiliary Territorial Service) at Camberley. 'She took immense pride in the fact that she was doing what other girls of her age had to do', wrote Crawfie, 'and apart from coming back to Windsor to sleep, she kept strictly to the routine of the mess, taking her turn with others as duty officer, doing inspections, and working really hard on the maintenance of cars.' But perhaps the most important thing she learned was all the hard work that went on before a visit from the Princess Royal. 'Now I realise what must happen when Papa and Mummie go anywhere. That's something I shall never forget.'

Scarcely had she finished her training when the war ended in 1945. On VE Day crowds surged to Buckingham Palace to acclaim the royal family for their part in the victory. After many balcony appearances the King encouraged his daughters to slip out with an escort of young officers to join the excited crowds below. He wanted them to experience at first hand the drama of the occasion for he felt the war had robbed them of many youthful pleasures: 'Poor darlings,' he wrote in his diary that night, 'they have never had any fun yet.'

Princess Elizabeth was nineteen, out of childhood, when the war ended, and Princess Margaret at fifteen was growing up fast. The King, however, liked to think of them still as children and would not agree to an engagement between Philip and Elizabeth, though the minds of the young couple were unalterably made up. Preparations were afoot for a trip to South Africa and the King was anxious that, perhaps for the first and last time, all four of them would go together. Princess Margaret was thrilled with the adventure and with the chance of new clothes after years of austerity but Princess Elizabeth was unhappy to be leaving Prince Philip behind. When they returned after a gruelling four-month tour, the King could resist his daughter's entreaties no longer. She married Prince Philip in Westminster Abbey in November 1947, aged twenty-one. The chief bridesmaid was of course her younger sister. Writing to Princess Elizabeth after the wedding, the King echoed the sadness of another father, the Prince Consort, who had lost his elder daughter to her husband nearly a hundred years before.

I have watched you grow up all these years with pride under the skilful direction of Mummy, who as you know is the most marvellous person in the World in my eyes, and I can, I know, always count on you, and now Philip, to help us in our work. Your leaving us has left a great blank in our lives but do remember that your old home is still yours and do come back to it as much and as often as possible. I can see that you are sublimely happy with Philip which is right but don't forget us is the wish of

Your ever loving & devoted
PAPA

6

Outward Bound

CHARLES
ANNE
ANDREW
EDWARD

May destiny, allotting what befalls,
    Grant to the newly-born this saving grace,
A guard more sure than ships and fortress-walls,
    The loyal love and service of a race.

John Masefield, 1948

*P*RINCESS Elizabeth hoped that her first child would arrive on her first wedding anniversary, but in fact it was six days earlier, on 14 November 1948, that a policeman announced to the waiting crowd: 'It's a boy!' There was no embarrassed Home Secretary waiting to verify this royal birth for King George VI had decided to dispense with the tradition. It had become established in the late seventeenth century as a reaction to rumours that a baby boy had been smuggled in a warming pan into the chamber of James II's queen, and had been passed off as the true heir. But even that most traditional monarch George VI saw no reason why over two hundred years later royal ladies should still have to tolerate politicians hovering outside their bedroom door.

Prince Philip had not been sitting patiently reading *Pilgrim's Progress*, like his wife's grandfather George V. While history was being made in a suite of rooms overlooking the Mall, he was playing squash and swimming in the Palace pool. But when the news came he leaped up the stairs three at a time and was by the Princess's bedside with a bouquet of carnations and roses when she came round from the anaesthetic.

The Prince was born soon after nine o'clock on a Sunday evening and

Princess Elizabeth and the Duke of Edinburgh with their month-old son, Prince Charles, after his christening.

the news brought crowds surging to the Palace to swell the numbers who had been eagerly waiting there all day. In Trafalgar Square the fountains ran blue for a boy and 4000 telegrams of congratulation reached the Palace the same night. At eleven pm the crowd was rewarded with a glimpse of Queen Mary driving in to see her first great-grandchild and when she left, an hour later, they were still as enthusiastic and noisy as ever. Eventually police vans had to disperse the crowd so that mother and baby could get some sleep.

On the following day pealing bells, booming cannon and fiery beacons welcomed the new Prince, who was fifth in descent from Queen Victoria and thirty-ninth from Alfred the Great. Celebrations went on all day and by evening another crowd had gathered to sing unsoothing lullabies outside Buckingham Palace. Princess Elizabeth was very well and radiantly happy. She wrote to a friend:

> Don't you think he is quite adorable? I still can't believe he is really mine, but perhaps that happens to new parents. Anyway, this particular boy's parents couldn't be more proud of him. It's wonderful to think, isn't it, that his arrival could give a bit of happiness to so many people, beside ourselves, at this time?

The family were divided as to which parent he most resembled but Queen Mary, leafing through old photographs, decided he took after his great-great-great grandfather Albert, Prince Consort. However, to everyone's surprise, Albert was not among the names given to the child. Ignoring Queen Victoria's rule that all male descendants should be named after her beloved consort, his parents decided to call him Charles Philip Arthur George. The choice of Charles was another surprise for the new prince would presumably one day become King Charles III and his two forebears of that name had suffered such distinctly chequered careers that the name could hardly be seen as a lucky one. However, the royal parents were not troubled by such considerations and made their choice, as the Palace stated, for 'personal and private reasons'.

The christening took place in the Music Room at Buckingham Palace, for the Chapel had been bombed during the war. The gold lily font made for the christening of the Princess Royal 108 years earlier was brought from Windsor and filled with water from the River Jordan, a custom which dated back to the Crusades. Among the close family circle gathered for the occasion were four surviving granddaughters of Queen Victoria, who had themselves worn the same lace christening robe. Queen Mary's present to the prince had yet older family associations: 'I gave the baby a silver gilt cup and cover which George III had given to a godson in 1780, so that I gave a present from my great-grandfather to my great-grandson 168 years later.'

Prince Charles was cared for by two nurses: Mrs Helen Lightbody and Miss Mabel Anderson. Mrs Lightbody, a strict though kindly nanny, had been recommended by the Duchess of Gloucester, so she was accustomed to royal circles. Miss Anderson, on the other hand, had advertised in a 'Situations Wanted' column and was amazed to find herself engaged by the royal nursery. The enormous pram which had been used for the little Princesses was wheeled out of storage, and Prince Charles still remembers lying in its vastness, with high sides all around him. In the New Year he went with the family to Sandringham, and then back to Buckingham Palace until July, when Clarence House was at last ready for his parents to move in to. It was only just across the Mall from the Palace but it was a home of their own.

The private gardens at the back of the house led on to St James's Park and here the baby, trailed discreetly by detectives, was often taken for an airing. Sometimes he would visit his great-grandmother across the park at Marlborough House, and one of his earliest memories is of Queen Mary sitting with upright posture in her chair, surrounded by all the bric-a-brac of her collections.

Prince Philip was still pursuing his naval career and before Prince Charles was a year old his father had been sent to sea, based on Malta. After her son's birthday Princess Elizabeth went out to join her husband and the little Prince spent Christmas with his grandparents and Aunt Margaret. But he was not to be the sole centre of attention for much longer, for Princess Elizabeth was pregnant again and on 15 August 1950 a baby sister was born at Clarence House. She was christened Anne Elizabeth Alice Louise, her first name being the one vetoed by George V when it was proposed for Princess Margaret.

With their father so much at sea, the mainstay of the children's life was their mother, who, though back in a whirl of public engagements, always set aside time for them. They did not go to her bedroom first thing, as she and her sister had done with their parents, but played in the nursery till nine o'clock and then saw their mother for half an hour. After tea she would join them in the nursery for more games before bathing them and putting them to bed herself. On her marriage she had looked forward to at least a decade of family life before she would be called to succeed her father on the throne, but even before Prince Charles was born the King's health had begun to fail. However, he did recover well from an operation in March 1950 to ease blood constriction in his leg, and by Christmas he was again enjoying the company of his grandchildren at Sandringham. Princess Elizabeth was away with her husband in Malta when the King wrote to her: 'Charles is too sweet, stumping around the room. We shall love having him at Sandringham. He is the fifth generation to live there and I hope he will get to like the place.'

But the improvement was short-lived, for the King had developed lung cancer. Sadly facing the inevitable, Prince Philip relinquished his naval command to help his wife with the increase in royal duties. In October 1951 the Prince and Princess left for a tour of North America, missing their son's third birthday in November. He spent the day with his grandparents at Buckingham Palace and has retained just one memory of his grandfather as he sat beside him on the sofa to have his picture taken. The resulting photograph of the dying King and the future King has always stood on the desk of Queen Elizabeth II.

Scarcely had Charles and Anne welcomed their parents home from America, before they were off again in January on the Commonwealth tour which had originally been planned for the King. The royal children were in the nursery at Sandringham only a week later when Queen Elizabeth came to tell them that Grandpa had gone away suddenly and that Mama and Papa were coming back. Prince Charles was too young to take in the full meaning of the tragedy but he was upset to see everyone in tears and gently urged the Queen, 'Don't cry, granny.'

He was now Duke of Cornwall, Duke of Rothesay, Earl of Carrick and Baron of Renfrew, Lord of the Isles and Great Steward of Scotland. 'That's me, Mummy,' he would cry as he heard his name mentioned in church, but his parents were in no hurry to make him aware of his destiny. To everyone in the Palace he was simply 'Charles', and the interest of crowds was so much part of life that he took it for granted. When asked years later to pinpoint the moment he first realised he was no ordinary mortal, Prince Charles said there was no sudden awakening: 'I think it's something that dawns on you with the most ghastly inexorable sense. I didn't suddenly wake up in my pram one day and say "Yippee". . . .'

Nevertheless as preparations for his mother's coronation got under way it must have been obvious to the young Prince that his mother was set apart from other people. The new Queen thought he was too young to take the solemn oath of allegiance that tradition demanded and indeed she decided against taking him to the Abbey at all, but the Prince so begged to see her crowned that she relented. After the main procession had passed on its way Prince Charles was arrayed in a white satin suit and

King George VI with his grandson Prince Charles. This is one of the Queen's
favourite family photographs.

taken by back streets to a side door of the Abbey. He arrived just as his mother was about to be anointed with oil, and in the midst of this solemn moment the Queen found time to give her son a reassuring smile. The Prince watched eagerly, full of questions for his grandmother beside him, and he was allowed to stay until the actual crowning had taken place. Back at the Palace he and his sister joined their parents on the balcony and looked down for the first time on the sea of madly cheering faces below.

Prince Charles has retained only the vaguest memory of that great day but Princess Anne remembers clearly that she was 'full of sisterly fury at being left behind'. She always minded being the younger one and strove in everything to catch up with her elder brother. They were totally different in character: Anne was tough, wilful and obstinate, Charles was sweet, shy and biddable. From an early age he displayed great considera-tion for others and was very well-mannered. It was no hardship for him to bow politely to Queen Mary while Anne, on the other hand, would steadfastly ignore instructions to curtsey to her great-grandmother. When she discovered that the Palace sentries had to present arms each time she passed them, she would go backwards and forwards for the pleasure of seeing them do it. Such a pastime would have embarrassed Prince Charles.

Soon after Charles's fifth birthday his parents set off on the long tour of the Commonwealth which had been interrupted by the King's death. They were away for over five months – an eternity to such young chil-dren. Charles and Anne knew, though, that there was a good reason for this long absence. 'Mummy has an important job to do,' Charles told a friend. He pointed out Australia on the globe: 'She's down here.' Towards the end of the tour the children prepared with great excitement to travel out on the new royal yacht *Britannia* to meet their parents' ship at Tobruk. The royal yacht was specially equipped with a sandpit and a slide, and four naval ratings were assigned the unenviable task of making sure the royal children were not lost overboard. After a merry week at Malta with their great-uncle, Lord Mountbatten, they were reunited with their parents and sailed back all together on *Britannia*. It was a grand homecoming; the royal yacht came right up the Thames to the Pool of London and there the family transferred into a stately barge and glided up river to a tumultuous welcome at Westminster.

With the excitement over and family life resumed, it was time for Prince Charles to begin proper lessons. He had already learned to ride, and to dance, but he had not progressed very far with reading or writing. His

Princess Anne was never particularly fond of dolls but she had to be photographed with them.

governess was Miss Catherine Peebles, nicknamed 'Mispy', who had taught the Duchess of Kent's two younger children. The Queen recognised that Charles was a very nervous child and so she decided it would not be a good idea to bring in other children to share his classes. Miss Peebles found him intelligent and interested but very sensitive to criticism: 'If you raised your voice to him he would draw back into his shell and for a time you would be able to do nothing with him.' He showed particular aptitude for history, geography and painting but shared his mother's blind spot for mathematics.

The Queen and the Duke of Edinburgh wanted their children to grow up as normally as possible and for this reason they hoped to send Prince Charles to school. They lowered him very gently into the shallow end by sending him for afternoons only to join the boys of Hill House private day school at Knightsbridge. After a term playing football – not very enthusiastically – Prince Charles was considered ready for a full school day. The first day of term passed off uneventfully but on the second he had to run the gauntlet of reporters and sightseers. On the third day the crowd was so large that the Queen's press secretary had to ring round all the newspaper editors to get the press hounds recalled before Charles could make his way to school. At last, however, public interest died down and he settled not unhappily into the school routine. It was after all only a day school and by four o'clock he was back in the bosom of the family.

Setting off in September 1957 to a boarding school was a very different matter. As he travelled south from Balmoral with his mother, Charles shuddered at the prospect in store. He was bound for his father's old prep school, Cheam, near the Hampshire Downs, where it was hoped sixty-five acres of grounds would shield him from prying eyes. The few days after his arrival Charles remembered as the most miserable of his life. He stood in the playground, a forlorn solitary figure, watching the games going on all around him but unable to join in. The other boys were too inhibited to make the normal overtures of friendship and to cover their embarrassment they ignored him. At night there was only a hard wooden bed in a roomful of strangers with no privacy for tears. It seems unlikely that either George and Eddy joining *Britannia* or Edward and Bertie starting at Osborne suffered quite as much as this modern Prince. True the naval environment was much tougher than Cheam School but they had been twelve or thirteen when they left home, whereas Prince Charles was only eight.

To add to his problems, the interest of the press was unrelenting. In the first term stories about him appeared in the newspapers on no less than sixty-eight occasions; even the school barber was reported to be in the pay of journalists. During the Christmas holidays the Queen's press secretary arranged a meeting with all the newspaper editors and explained what the constant harassment was doing to the school. Unless it stopped Prince Charles would have to return to solitary lessons at Buckingham Palace. Belatedly repentant the editors switched the spotlight off Cheam and, apart from occasional invasions by foreign reporters, the school ran normally again.

Gradually the Prince settled more easily into school life, but it was with resignation rather than enjoyment. There are many sensitive boys for whom school remains always something of a penance, and he was one of them. Indeed it was much worse for him, for as well as suffering from a lack of privacy, he was lonely. There was no one whose experience of life was anything like his, and even if people were interested he dare not confide in them. Prince Philip once summed up the inevitable aloneness of royal children: 'The children soon discover that it's much safer to unburden yourself to a member of the family than just to a friend. . . . You see, you're never quite sure . . . a small indiscretion can lead to all sorts of difficulties.' Charles's parents viewed his unhappiness with great concern but they felt to withdraw him from school would be a terrible defeat. He had to learn to survive the pressures of school if he were later to support the burden of kingship.

Back in Buckingham Palace Princess Anne was longing to go to school and fretted at her narrow existence. Although the photographers loved to take pictures of her pushing prams, she was never very interested in dolls and preferred her mother's old rocking horse to any other toy. When she began lessons several other little girls were brought in to join her class but, as she later admitted, she 'wasn't actually a very popular person' for she fought with the boys and disliked the girls on principle. Although she was very like her father in arrogance and bluntness, they had a very good relationship and he took as much trouble to introduce her to all his outdoor pursuits as he did with Charles. Her mother taught her to ride at the age of three, but it was her father who taught her to swim, and by the age of six she could dive from his shoulders. At nine years old, under his guidance, she had learned to drive a bubble car along the private roads at Windsor. Due to Prince Philip's insistence Princess Anne did not grow up in the neat kilts and pretty dresses that her mother had worn, but in hard-wearing trousers and sweaters. Dressed up as a bridesmaid for a royal wedding she could look every inch a princess, but she much preferred mucking out the stables or crewing for her father in a sailing dinghy.

When Princess Anne was nine, and Prince Charles eleven, the Queen presented them with a baby brother: Andrew Albert Christian Edward. The Queen had always wanted more than two children but with her father's death, the coronation, and her new role, she had been too busy to take time off for child-bearing. Prince Andrew was the first child born to a reigning monarch since the birth of Beatrice to Queen Victoria, 103 years before. The Queen was delighted to have another boy for she was anxious to protect Anne from being second in succession: 'I don't want her to have the life of my sister Margaret' she told a friend.

From the outset Prince Andrew was a smiling, extrovert baby who grew into a lively and mischievous little boy. Nothing pleased him more than to tie together the laces on the boots of palace guardsmen or to hide whoopee cushions among his parents' armchairs. Though 'not always a little ray of sunshine', as the Queen said drily, he was a much more confident child than his elder brother, and fitted more easily into his father's educational programme.

Soon after Andrew's birth Prince Charles moved on to the second leg of this programme, Gordonstoun school in north Scotland. Again it was his father's old school and Prince Philip was very keen for Charles to go there, but ultimately the decision was left to him. 'My parents were marvellous in this way,' Prince Charles said later. 'They'd outline all the possibilities and in the end it was up to you. My father had a particularly strong influence and it was good for me. I had perfect confidence in his judgement.' So although he thought the school sounded 'pretty gruesome' he agreed to go there.

Given the sympathy the Queen and Duke felt for their children's problems, it seems surprising that they encouraged their diffident son to go to a tough school where his extrovert father had been a great success. However, it was certainly a long way for reporters to travel, and he was possibly no more unhappy than he would have been anywhere else. The Queen and her mother had favoured Eton but the Queen was usually to defer to her husband's judgement on their children's education for she felt his experience was so much wider than hers.

The first term at Gordonstoun was every bit as bad as the early days at Cheam. It was not so much the spartan conditions, or the exhausting expeditions, as the constant sense of being lonely in a crowd. The aim of the school was to build up the character of pupils with a combination of adventure and service. Looking back Prince Charles believes it was a good

Prince Charles walks to church from Cheam School.

The royal family after the birth of Prince Andrew in 1960.

system, but even now he doesn't claim he enjoyed it. One incident in his first year, when a reporter caught him drinking cherry brandy under age, left him with particularly bitter memories and a colossal loss of confidence. He recalled it in a television interview years later:

Well, I can say I thought it was the end of the earth. I was all ready to pack my bags and leave for Siberia or wherever. But in fact, all it was was that I was on a cruise from Gordonstoun in the school yacht and we went to Stornoway and I went to a hotel to have a meal and while we were waiting for the meal a lot of people were looking in the windows, and so I thought 'I can't bear this any more'. And went off somewhere else and the only other place was the bar. Having never been into a bar before the first thing I thought of doing was having a drink, of course. It seemed the most sensible thing. And being terrified not knowing what to do I said the first drink that came into my head, which happened to be cherry brandy, because I'd drunk it before when it was cold, out shooting. And hardly had I taken a sip when the whole world exploded round my ears. That's all.

Unfortunately the Palace first denied the story and then retracted their denial, so the whole trivial incident gained unnecessary publicity. It was a hard lesson for a fourteen-year-old boy to learn, that even in the remote Outer Hebrides there were people waiting to catch him out in the slightest misdemeanour. And if the publicity were not sufficient punishment, he was also reduced to the ranks at school after he had just begun to progress upwards in the hierarchy.

In this same year, 1963, Princess Anne at last achieved her long-felt desire to go to school. She had greatly enjoyed guide camps that summer and the previous one, and if she could get on so well with a mixed bunch of Londoners she would surely be happy among the girls at Benenden School in Kent. She was much more fortunate than Charles in her early days because at Benenden all new girls were allocated a 'house mother' and gravitated naturally into the house mother's group of friends. Princess Anne described her circle as 'a caustic lot who knew exactly what they thought about other people and saved one a lot of embarrassment'. She was not exactly homesick but she found 'the amount of people and the noise was staggering'. Happy in her own company, this was one aspect of school which she found a constant trial. Like her elder brother she was trailed everywhere by a detective, who sometimes attracted more attention than she did. Once he was watching her at a riding lesson and his concentration caught the attention of men unloading a van. 'What's that man watching you for?' they enquired. 'You royalty or something?' When she told them the truth they refused to believe it.

Anne settled down well at school, worked just hard enough at her

The six-month-old Prince Andrew laughing with his grandmother, the Queen Mother.

lessons to get by, and took six 'O' levels and two 'A' levels without much trouble. She played badminton, went swimming and rock climbing, sang in the choir, struggled with the oboe and acted in the Drama Club, but her chief effort and enthusiasm was centred on riding. She kept her pony High Jinks at a nearby riding school and began to compete in gymkhanas and horse trials. In 1968, the year she left Benenden, she was given her first horse and finished a pleased seventh in the novice class at the Windsor Horse Trials.

In the school holidays Charles, Anne, Andrew and baby Edward (born 1964) enjoyed a happy family life in one of the several royal homes. Buckingham Palace had a mere eleven acres of lawns, trees and lakes to play in but at Sandringham and Balmoral there was infinite space – and reasonable privacy in which to enjoy it. Prince Philip devoted hours to teaching them all the outdoor sports he enjoyed so much, such as sailing, riding, fishing and swimming. 'I've always tried to help them master at least one thing', Prince Philip said, 'because as soon as a child feels self-confidence in one area, it spills over into all the others.' Prince Charles had a great admiration for his father and tried hard to emulate all his achievements, but he shared his mother's wit and sensitivity and as he grew older they became increasingly close. He was also a great admirer of Lord Mountbatten, his father's uncle, and called him his honorary grandfather. Problems that he found difficult to discuss with his parents could always be taken to Lord Mountbatten, or to his grandmother Queen Elizabeth the Queen Mother. 'Ever since I can remember', he wrote in 1979, 'my grandmother has been the most wonderful example of fun, laughter, warmth, infinite security and, above all else, exquisite taste in so many things.'

Towards the end of his time at Gordonstoun Prince Charles began to find his feet. He passed five 'O' levels at the first try and mathematics in the following year. He became deeply interested in archaeology, learned the cello, became a prefect and starred in the school's production of *Macbeth*. But it was two terms in Australia in 1966 that really gave him confidence and maturity. He was sent to Timbertop, an outpost of Geelong School, where boys were taught self-reliance amid the great gum forests two hundred miles north of Melbourne. Gordonstoun was a soft billet compared with Timbertop, but somehow Charles fitted in much better with the Australian boys. They were interested in him, but quite unawed, and after only a few days he felt he belonged. 'The most wonderful experience I've ever had,' he later described his time at Timbertop, and he meant not just the excitement of hikes penetrating into deepest

Prince Charles go-karting with the five-year-old Prince Edward.

The new generation: Master Peter Phillips with his royal grandparents, his mother and his three uncles. The photograph was taken in 1979 on the Queen's thirty-second wedding anniversary.

Australia but the novel sense of being accepted for what he was, not who he was. While he was over there he went to visit New Guinea and had a wonderful reception from feather-clad, drum-beating natives:

and then we arrived at the entrance to the village and the drums stopped and the whole village were assembled there and for some unknown reason they suddenly started to sing 'God Save the Queen' and it was the most moving, touching thing I have ever experienced, I think, to see these native people, miles from Britain, singing the National Anthem.

Back at Gordonstoun, his last year passed pleasantly working for 'A' levels, playing his cello and carrying out the duties of the guardian (head boy). But he looked forward to leaving school, particularly now that Timbertop had given him the confidence to face the outside world. In the autumn of 1967 he arrived at Trinity College Cambridge – the first heir to the throne actually to qualify for university entrance. In his second year came his worst ordeal so far: eight weeks at Aberystwyth University learning Welsh followed by his Investiture as Prince of Wales at Caernarvon Castle. The Welsh Nationalists strongly objected to the Investiture, and to his presence at Aberystwyth, but once he came to live among them, protest rapidly died down. 'He came and saw and conquered the Welsh,' Prince Philip remarked proudly to a friend.

The Investiture itself was a grand spectacle, but most moving of all was the Queen's obvious pride in her eldest son as she presented him to the Welsh people. For the Prince the ceremony marked the end of childhood; the years of preparation were over and he had entered public life.

Princess Anne too was now becoming a public figure. She had left Benenden in 1968 with no clear idea of what to do next, except to carry on with her riding. Her parents feared this would not prove satisfying for long but the Princess's success – she was voted Sportswoman of the Year in 1971, delighted them. They were pleased too when through her interest in horses she met and married Mark Phillips. With the disastrous marriage of Princess Margaret in the forefront of their minds, they cared desperately that their daughter should choose the right man.

Andrew and Edward were growing up with many fewer problems than their elders. Andrew could on occasions be aggressive and rude but he bounced through prep school and into Gordonstoun with none of the anguish of his elder brother. The school had softened up considerably since Charles's time; the cold showers had been abolished and girl students had been admitted – both changes which Andrew greatly appreciated. One of the masters described him as 'a very tough and independent young fellow. He has no time for sycophants. On the other hand, if anyone tries to take the mickey out of him he doesn't hesitate to fight back. He's good – just as good – with verbalistics as he is with his fists.' His two terms in Lakefield College – the Canadian equivalent of Timbertop – in 1977 proved a broadening experience and rubbed off some of his aggressive corners. When he returned to Gordonstoun in the autumn of 1977 he was joined by Prince Edward, and did what he could to ease the first term of his younger brother. In 1979 he passed his 'A' levels and entered the Navy to train as a helicopter pilot.

The Queen was anxious that her two younger sons should enjoy more private lives than their elders and as a result very little is yet known about Prince Edward's tastes or abilities. He was a charming page boy at Princess Anne's wedding, a keen spectator of the Montreal Olympics, and rode with his grandmother in the Silver Jubilee procession, but apart from such occasions his public appearances are few. He is thought to be the most quiet and contemplative one of the family, fond of serene pleasures like fishing and birdwatching. Perhaps he will be able to break the royal tradition of a career in the services and strike out in a new direction.

Whatever his choice, he will not escape the bonds of his royal birth. The privileges and responsibilities of his position will follow him wherever he goes. Why then have his parents concentrated so hard on a 'normal' upbringing for their children, rather than a preparation for their very abnormal role? 'Training isn't necessary,' Prince Philip once said. 'They do on-the-job training, so to speak, and learn the trade, or business, or craft, just from being with us and watching us function, and seeing the whole organisation around us. They can't avoid it.

'What is much more difficult is bringing them up as people.'

Biographical Notes

1 THE CHILDREN OF QUEEN VICTORIA AND PRINCE ALBERT

Victoria Adelaide Mary Louise, Princess Royal and Empress of Germany. Called 'Vicky'. (1840–1901)
Married Prince Frederick William (Fritz) of Prussia in 1858. Four sons and four daughters. Her marriage was a happy one but her abilities and her liberal views earned her hostility in the rigid, authoritarian, anti-English German court. When her husband at last succeeded to the throne as Frederick III he was dying of throat cancer, and his wife was on terms of enmity with the all-powerful statesman Bismarck. After only three months as Empress, Vicky was left a widow and alienated from her arrogant eldest son, now William II (the Kaiser). After a long and painful illness she died of cancer in the same year as her mother; her last years were cheered only by the devotion of her younger daughters and the constant affection of her English family.

Albert Edward, Edward VII. Called 'Bertie'. (1841–1910)
Married Princess Alexandra of Denmark in 1863. Two sons and three daughters (see below). His many years as Prince of Wales were passed in a whirl of amusements and infidelities,

with no encouragement from his mother to play a part in affairs of state. In 1901 he ascended the throne and surprised his critics with his application and astuteness. His talent for personal diplomacy earned him the title 'Edward the Peacemaker', and he revived much of the pomp and pageantry of royalty which Victoria in her widowhood had avoided. His charm and geniality won him widespread affection.

Alice Maud Mary, Grand-duchess of Hesse-Darmstadt. (1843–78)
Married Prince Frederick William Louis of Hesse in 1862. Five daughters and two sons. Although devoted to her husband she did not find in him an intellect which matched her own, or in the small German court enough outlets for her reforming energies. She was particularly involved in improving nursing standards and in the Franco-Prussian war she herself cared for the wounded at Darmstadt hospital. She was also a patron of the arts. In 1878 she nursed her children through diphtheria but her youngest daughter Mary died and Alice picked up the infection while trying to comfort her son. She died on 14 December 1878, the seven-

teenth anniversary of her father's death, aged only thirty-five. Queen Victoria took the closest interest in bringing up her motherless children: one daughter, Alix, married Tsar Nicholas II and another, Victoria, was the grandmother of Prince Philip, Duke of Edinburgh.

Alfred Ernest Albert, Duke of Edinburgh, Duke of Saxe-Coburg and Gotha. Called 'Affie'. (1844–1900)
Married the Grand Duchess Marie, only daughter of Tsar Alexander II in 1874. One son and four daughters. He made a successful career in the Royal Navy, rising to Admiral of the Fleet. In 1893 he left the Navy to succeed his father's brother as Duke of Saxe-Coburg and Gotha.

Helena Augusta Victoria, Princess of Schleswig-Holstein. Called 'Lenchen'. (1846–1923)
Married Prince Christian of Schleswig-Holstein in 1866. Two sons and two daughters. Prince Christian was much older than his wife, and very dull, but the marriage was nevertheless a happy one. The Princess devoted much time to good works, in particular to the Princess Christian nursing home at Windsor.

Louise Caroline Alberta, Duchess of Argyll. (1848–1939)
She was the most beautiful and most gifted, artistically, of Queen Victoria's daughters. In 1871 she married John Campbell, Marquess of Lorne, later Duke of Argyll; there were no children. From 1878–83 her husband was governor-general of Canada and she

accompanied him overseas. The marriage was not a happy one. Back in England she supported many worthy causes, particularly the higher education of women, and made her home at Kensington Palace a rendezvous for artists and sculptors.

Arthur William Patrick Albert, Duke of Connaught. (1850–1942)
Married Princess Louisa of Prussia in 1879. One son and two daughters. He achieved his childhood ambition of becoming a soldier and industriously pursued a military career, becoming a field-marshal in 1902. From 1911–16 he was governor-general of Canada. His life, though crowned with honours, was saddened by the fact that his wife, son and a daughter all predeceased him.

Leopold George Duncan Albert, Duke of Albany. (1853–84)
Married Princess Helen of Waldeck-Pyrmont in 1882. One daughter and one son (born posthumously). The Prince's life was a long struggle to pursue a normal life despite his haemophilia. He was the cleverest of Victoria's sons, and very dear to her, though he frequently quarrelled with her attempts to restrict his life. He attended Oxford University and took a great interest in educational causes. He died after a fall while on holiday at Cannes.

Beatrice May Victoria Feodore, Princess of Battenberg. (1857–1944)
Married Prince Henry of Battenberg in 1885. Three sons and one daughter. Queen Victoria only agreed to her

youngest daughter's marriage on condition that the Battenbergs made their home with her, and her old age was much enlivened by her son-in-law and the Battenberg grandchildren. But Prince Henry volunteered to join the Ashanti expedition of 1895 and died on his way home in January the following year. Princess Beatrice continued to live with her mother until the Queen's death, after which she divided her time between Kensington Palace and Carisbrooke Castle. Queen Victoria's private journals were bequeathed to her and she spent many years copying out the parts she considered fit for posterity; the originals she destroyed.

2 THE CHILDREN OF EDWARD VII AND QUEEN ALEXANDRA

Albert Victor Christian Edward, Duke of Clarence and Avondale. Called 'Eddy'. (1864–92)
After naval training and a three-year cruise on HMS *Bacchante* he spent some time at Trinity College, Cambridge. In 1886 he was sent to Aldershot and joined the 10th Hussars. He showed no aptitude for an army career, and no interest in anything but dissipation. A marriage was arranged with his cousin Princess Mary of Teck but six weeks before the wedding he died of pneumonia at Sandringham in January 1892.

Frederick Ernest Albert George, George V. (1865–1936)
Prince George pursued a naval career until 1892, when the death of his elder brother made him his father's heir. He was created Duke of York, left the Royal Navy, and married his brother's bereaved fiancée, Princess Mary of Teck. It was a very happy marriage and six children were born to them (*see below*). Until the death of Queen Victoria George led the life of a country squire in York Cottage on the Sandringham estate. When his father became Edward VII, he began to take a more active role and made successful tours of Australia and India. He became king in 1910. He was not a clever man, but his indefatigable sense of duty, particularly in the First World War, earned him respect and affection, which expressed itself in the great enthusiasm of his Silver Jubilee in 1935.

Louise Victoria Alexandra Dagmar, Princess Royal, Duchess of Fife. (1867–1931)
Married in 1889 Alexander Duff, Earl of Fife, who was created Duke on his marriage. Two daughters. In 1911 the whole family was shipwrecked on the way to Egypt; they escaped safely but the Duke died two months later of fever at Aswan. Though created Princess Royal in 1905 the Duchess took almost no part at all in public affairs but lived a retired life both before and after her husband's death.

Victoria Alexandra Olga Mary. (1868–1935)
She was the most intelligent of Edward VII's daughters but her mother kept her at home as a companion and she was never encouraged to marry. The Princess was fifty-seven before her mother's death enabled her to lead an independent life at Coppins, Iver, in Buckinghamshire. She remained on

closely affectionate terms with her brother King George v, and grief at her death hastened his own.

Maud Charlotte Mary Victoria, Queen of Norway. (1869–1938)
Married Prince Christian Frederick

Charles of Denmark in 1896 and bore him one son, Olav, in 1903. She kept an English home at Appleton near Sandringham and visited it often. In 1905 her husband was elected to the throne of Norway, taking the name Haakon VII.

3 THE CHILDREN OF GEORGE V AND QUEEN MARY

Edward Albert Christian George Andrew Patrick David, Edward VIII, Duke of Windsor. Called 'David'. (1895–1972)
Educated at Osborne, Dartmouth and Magdalen College, Oxford. Served in the army in the First World War. As Prince of Wales he made several successful overseas tours and became immensely popular. Hoped to bring fresh air into the monarchy when he succeeded his father in 1936, but had to abdicate within a year because he wished to marry Wallis Simpson, a twice-divorced American. Lived abroad the rest of his life, and served as governor of the Bahamas during the Second World War. No children.

Albert Frederick Arthur George, Duke of York, George VI. Called 'Bertie'. (1896–1952)
Educated at Osborne, Dartmouth and Trinity College, Cambridge. Served in the Grand Fleet at the battle of Jutland (1916) and afterwards in the RAF. As Duke of York he was keenly interested in industry and boys' camps. He married Lady Elizabeth Bowes-Lyon in 1923. Two daughters (see below). In 1936 he unexpectedly became king on his elder brother's abdication. Hampered by a speech impediment and lack of training for his role, he soon found

his feet and worked indomitably throughout the war, raising morale with his broadcasts, visits to troops and to bombed areas, and happy family life. Never robust, he wore himself out and died of coronary thrombosis at the age of only fifty-six.

Victoria Alexandra Alice Mary, Princess Royal, Countess of Harewood. Called 'Mary'. (1897–1965)
Educated at home, trained as a nurse and worked at Great Ormond Street Hospital. Married in 1922 Henry, Viscount Lascelles, Earl of Harewood, who was sixteen years her senior. The Princess divided her life between bringing up their two sons and carrying out public duties.

Henry William Frederick Albert, Duke of Gloucester. (1900–74)
Educated at Eton and Sandhurst. Tried to pursue a career in the army but was frustrated by his royal status, which prevented him going to politically sensitive areas such as Ireland, Egypt and India. He married Lady Alice Montagu-Douglas-Scott and had two sons. After the abdication of Edward VIII he became Regent Designate until his niece came of age. Although a retiring man by nature he often represented

the sovereign abroad and was governor-general of Australia from 1945–7.

George Edward Alexander Edmund, Duke of Kent. (1902–42)
Educated at Dartmouth for the Royal Navy, but was unhappy at sea and left to work at the Foreign Office. He married Princess Marina of Greece and had two sons and a daughter. He was killed on active service in the RAF when his flying boat crashed in Scotland. He was the most clever and artistic of George V's children.

John Charles Francis (1905–19)
In early childhood the Prince developed epilepsy, which retarded his development. At the age of eleven he was given a separate establishment at Wood Farm on the Sandringham Estate. He died there two years later.

4 THE CHILDREN OF GEORGE VI AND QUEEN ELIZABETH

Elizabeth Alexandra Mary, Elizabeth II. Called 'Lilibet'. (Born 1926)
Educated at home. Married Prince Philip of Greece, Duke of Edinburgh, in 1947 and bore him three sons and a daughter (see below). Succeeded to the throne in 1952.

Margaret Rose, Countess of Snowdon. (Born 1930)
Educated at home. Wished to marry Group-Captain Peter Townsend but his divorced status made this impossible. In 1960 married Antony Armstrong-Jones, a photographer, who was created Earl of Snowdon. A son, Viscount Linley, and daughter, Lady Sarah. The marriage ended in 1978.

5 THE CHILDREN OF ELIZABETH II AND PRINCE PHILIP

Charles Philip Arthur George, Prince of Wales. (Born 1948)
Educated at Gordonstoun, Timbertop in Australia and Trinity College, Cambridge. Investiture as Prince of Wales at Caernarvon Castle in 1969. Served in the Royal Navy 1971–6. Resigned in order to spend more time on public engagements.

Anne Elizabeth Alice Louise. (Born 1950)
Educated at home and at Benenden School in Kent. Chosen Sportswoman of the Year for her riding successes in 1971. Married Captain Mark Phillips in 1973. A son, Peter, born in 1978.

Andrew Albert Christian Edward. (Born 1960)
Educated at Gordonstoun and Lakefield College in Canada. Joined Royal Navy in 1979.

Edward Antony Richard Louis. (Born 1964)
Now at Gordonstoun.

Select Bibliography

CHAPTERS 1 AND 2

Aston, Sir George G. *H.R.H. The Duke of Connaught and Strathearn* (London, 1929)

Bennett, Daphne *Queen Victoria's Children* (Gollancz, 1980)

Bennett, Daphne *Vicky: Princess Royal of England and German Empress* (Collins, 1971).

Benson, A. C., and Viscount Esher *The Letters of Queen Victoria, A Selection from Her Majesty's Correspondence: First series 1837–61* (John Murray, 1907)

Bolitho, H. *The Prince Consort and his Brother: Two hundred new letters* (London, 1933)

Broadley, A. M. *The Boyhood of a Great King 1841–58* (London, 1906)

Duff, David *The Shy Princess* (Evans Brothers, 1958)

Duff, David *Hessian Tapestry* (Muller, 1967)

Epton, Nina *Queen Victoria and her Daughters* (Weidenfeld & Nicolson, 1971)

Fulford, Roger *The Prince Consort* (Macmillan, 1949)

Fulford, Roger (ed.) *Dearest Child: Letters between Queen Victoria and the Princess Royal 1858–61* (Evans Brothers, 1958)

Fulford, Roger (ed.) *Dearest Mama: Letters between Queen Victoria and the Crown Princess of Prussia 1861–64* (Evans Brothers, 1968)

Longford, Elizabeth *Victoria R.I.* (Weidenfeld & Nicolson, 1964)

Lyttelton, Lady Sarah *Correspondence 1787–1870*, ed. Hon. Mrs Hugh Wyndham (John Murray, 1912)

Magnus, Philip *King Edward the Seventh* (John Murray, 1964)

Stanley, Lady Augusta *Letters etc 1849–63*, ed. by A. V. Baillie and H. Bolitho (Gerald Howe, 1927)

Victoria, Queen *Leaves from the Journal of Our Life in the Highlands* (Smith, Elder & Co., 1868); *More Leaves* etc. (1884)

Warner, Marina *Queen Victoria's Sketchbook* (Macmillan, 1979)

CHAPTER 3

Alice, Princess *For My Grandchildren* (Evans Brother, 1966)

Battiscombe, Georgina *Queen Alexandra* (Constable, 1969)

Dalton, J. N. (ed.) *Cruise of HMS Bacchante 1879–82*, 2 vols (Macmillan, 1886)

Select Bibliography

Gore, John *King George V: a personal memoir* (John Murray, 1941)
Marie-Louise, Princess *My Memories of Six Reigns* (Evans Brother, 1956)
Nicolson, Harold *George V: his life and reign* (Constable, 1952)
Vincent, James E. *H.R.H. The Duke of Clarence and Avondale* (London, 1893)
Wakeford, Geoffrey *The Princesses Royal* (Hale, 1973)

CHAPTER 4

Carey, M. C. *Princess Mary* (Nisbet & Co., 1922)
Donaldson, Frances *Edward VIII* (Weidenfeld & Nicolson, 1974)
Frankland, Noble *Prince Henry, Duke of Gloucester* (Weidenfeld & Nicolson, 1980)
Graham, Evelyn *Princess Mary, Viscount Lascelles* (Hutchinson, 1929)
Kinloch Cooke, C. *A Memoir of H.R.H. Princess Mary Adelaide, Duchess of Teck* (John Murray, 1900)
Mackenzie, Compton *The Windsor Tapestry* (Rich and Cowan, 1938)
Pope-Hennessy, James *Queen Mary* (Allen & Unwin, 1954)
Tschumi, Gabriel *Royal Chef: Recollections of Life in Royal Households* (William Kimber, 1954)
Wheeler-Bennett, John *The Life and Reign of George VI* (Macmillan, 1958)
Windsor, Duke of *A King's Story* (Cassell, 1951)
Windsor, Duke of *A Family Album* (Cassell, 1960)

CHAPTER 5

Airlie, Mabell, Countess of *Thatched with Gold* (Hutchinson, 1962)
Asquith, Lady Cynthia *The King's Daughters* (Hutchinson, 1937)
Asquith, Lady Cynthia *Haply I may remember* (James Barrie, 1950)
Channon, Sir Henry *Chips: The Diaries of Sir Henry Channon*, ed. Robert Rhodes James (Weidenfeld & Nicolson, 1967)
Crawford, Marion *The Little Princesses* (Cassell, 1950)
Crawford, Marion *Princess Margaret* (George Newnes, 1953)
Chance, Michael *Our Princesses and their Dogs* (John Murray, 1936)
Lacey, Robert *Majesty* (Hutchinson, 1977)
Longford, Elizabeth *The Royal House of Windsor* (Weidenfeld & Nicolson, 1974)
Ring, Anne *The Story of Princess Elizabeth* (John Murray, 1930)
Synge, V. M. *Royal Guides* (Girl Guides Association, 1948)

CHAPTER 6

Alexandra, Queen of Yugoslavia *Prince Philip: A Family Portrait* (Hodder and Stoughton, 1960)
Campbell, Judith *Anne: Portrait of a Princess* (Cassell, 1970)

Select Bibliography

Cathcart, Helen *Her Majesty* (W. H. Allen, 1962)

Duff, David *Mother of the Queen* (Muller, 1965)

Edgar, Donald *The Queen's Children* (Arthur Barker, 1978)

Edgar, Donald *Prince Andrew* (Arthur Barker, 1980)

Holden, Antony *Charles, Prince of Wales* (Weidenfeld & Nicolson, 1980)

Morrah, Dermot *To Be a King* (Hutchinson, 1968)

Peacock, Lady Irene *The Queen and Her Children: An Authoritative Account* (Hutchinson, 1961)

Acknowledgements

The author and publisher would like to thank the following for permission to reproduce the illustrations in this book:

BBC Hulton Picture Library, 2, 105 *below*, 111, 113, 117, 123.
Reproduced by Gracious Permission of Her Majesty the Queen, 15 *above*, 21, 25, 29, 33, 35, 37, 41, 47, 49, 57, 61 *below*, 67, 75, 79, 85 *above*.
National Portrait Gallery, 23 *above*.
Controller of Her Majesty's Stationery Office (Crown copyright), 25.
Weidenfeld and Nicolson Archives, 53, 85 *below*, 89 *below*, 101 *below*, 127 *below*, *endpapers*.
Mansell Collection, 61 *above*, 63, 77, 89 *above*.
ILN Picture Library, 95.
Popperfoto, 101 *above*, 121.
Camera Club (photo by Marcus Adams), 105 *above*.
Keystone Press, 127 *above*.
The Press Association, 129, 131 *below*.
Fox Photos, 131 *above*.

INDEX

Abdication, the, 9, 106, 110
Airlie, Mabell, Countess of, 83, 94, 98
Albert, Prince Consort, 7, 11, 13, 14, 16–18, 19–22, 24, 26, 27, 30, 31, 34, 36, 38, 39, 40, 42–6, 54, 59, 60, 73, 74, 76, 80, 115, 118
Albert Victor, Prince, Duke of Clarence ('Eddy'), 10, 11, 54, 58, 59, 62, 64, 65, 66, 68–72; biographical note, 136
Alexandra, Queen, 46, 48, 51, 52, 54–6, 58–60, 62, 64, 66, 68–71, 76, 80, 82, 86, 92
Alfred, Prince, Duke of Edinburgh, 20, 28, 32, 36, 39, 42, 43, 45, 46, 55; biographical note, 135
Alice, Princess, 19, 20, 24, 28, 32, 34, 40, 42–6, 48, 58, 62, 74, 109; biographical note, 134
Alice, Princess, Duchess of Athlone, 82
Alix of Hesse ('Alicky'), later Tsarina, 73
Anderson, Mabel (nanny), 119
Andrew, Prince, 126, 130, 132, 133; biographical note, 138
Anne, Princess, 7, 10, 119, 121, 122, 125, 126, 127, 130, 132, 133; biographical note, 138
Arthur, Prince, Duke of Connaught, 27, 28, 32, 42, 45, 46, 48, 50; biographical note, 135
Augusta, Princess, Grand Duchess of Mecklenburg-Strelitz, 73, 78
Augusta, Princess of Prussia, later German Empress, 38, 40

Bacchante, HMS, 66, 68, 69
Balmoral, 34, 36, 39, 40, 42, 46, 59, 80, 86, 92, 109, 124

Barrie, Sir James, 102, 103, 112
Barrington, Lady Caroline, 28, 34
Battenberg, Prince Henry of, 51
Beatrice, Princess, 34, 40, 44–6, 48, 50, 51, 62, 64, 73; biographical note, 136
Benenden School, 128, 130, 132
Bill, Charlotte ('Lalla'), 78, 92
Birch, Henry, 24, 31
Britannia, HMS, 65, 66, 88
Britannia, royal yacht, 122, 124
Bruce, Colonel, 43, 46
Buckingham Palace, 26, 96, 97, 99, 106, 107, 108, 114, 118, 119, 120, 121, 125

Canning, Lady, 31
Channon, Sir Henry ('Chips'), 104, 112
Charles, Prince of Wales, 7, 9, 10, 11, 116, 118–22, 124–6, 130, 132; biographical note, 138
Charlotte, Princess, 13
Cheam School, 124, 125
Collingwood, HMS, 91
Crawford, Marion, 9, 99, 100, 103, 107, 109, 110, 112, 114

Dalton, John, 59, 62, 64, 65, 66, 68, 69, 70
Dartmouth Royal Naval College, 91, 109

Edinburgh, Duke of, see Philip, Prince
Eddy, see Albert Victor, Prince
Edward VII, King, biographical note, 134; childhood, 9, 12, 19, 22, 24, 28, 30–2, 36, 39, 42–6, 51; as father, 7, 52, 54, 55, 58–60, 62, 64, 66, 69; as grandfather, 73, 74, 78, 80, 81, 86

Edward VIII, Duke of Windsor, 8, 9, 11, 73, 74, 78, 80–3, 86, 87, 90, 91, 94, 98, 104; biographical note, 137
Edward, Prince, 130, 132, 133; biographical note, 138
Elizabeth II, Queen, childhood, 8, 9, 11, 92, 94, 96–8, 100, 102–4, 107–10, 112, 114, 115; as mother, 7, 116, 118–21, 124–6, 132; biographical note, 138
Elizabeth, Queen, the Queen Mother, 92–4, 96, 97, 99, 100, 103, 104, 107–9, 112, 119–21, 130
Elphinstone, Major, 46, 54
Ernst, Duke of Saxe-Coburg-Gotha, 14
Esher, Lord, 84, 87
Eugénie, Empress, 39

Finch, Frederick, 81, 86, 88
Frederick III, Emperor of Germany ('Fritz'), 30, 36, 40
Fuller, Charles, 59, 70, 81
Frogmore, 44, 82

George III, King, 118
George IV, King, 13, 31
George V, King, childhood, 10, 11, 55, 56, 58, 60, 62, 64–6, 68–71; as father, 73, 74, 80, 81–4, 87, 88, 90, 91, 92, 116; as grandfather, 94, 96–8, 104; biographical note, 136
George VI, King, childhood, 75, 76, 78, 80, 81, 84, 86–8, 90, 91, 92, 114; as father, 93, 94, 96–100, 103, 104, 106–10, 112, 115; as grandfather, 116, 119, 120; biographical note, 137
George II, King of Greece, 110
George, Prince, Duke of Kent, 10, 78, 83, 84, 90, 91; biographical note, 138

Gibbs, Frederick, 31, 43
Glamis Castle, 96, 98, 99
Gloucester, Duke of, *see*
 Henry, Prince
Gordonstoun School, 126,
 127, 130, 132, 133

Hansell, Henry, 81, 86, 88
Helena, Princess, 24, 32, 36,
 42, 45, 48, 50; biographical
 note, 135
Henry, Prince, Duke of
 Gloucester, 10, 78, 80, 84,
 86, 87, 90, 91; biographical
 note, 137
Hildyard, Miss, 22, 28
Hill House School, 124

Illustrious, HMS, 39
Investiture of Prince of
 Wales (1911), 90; (1969)
 132

John, Prince (son of Edward
 VII), 58
John, Prince (son of George
 V), 78, 90, 92; biographical
 note, 138

Kent, Victoria of
 Saxe-Coburg, Duchess
 of, 44
Kent, Duke of, *see* George,
 Prince
Knight, Clara ('Alah'), 96,
 97, 100
Knollys, Francis, 60, 68

Lehzen, Baroness, 17
Leopold I, King of Belgium,
 14, 16, 22
Leopold, Prince, Duke of
 Albany, 32, 34, 45, 46, 48,
 50
Leveson-Gower, Lady
 Rose, 98, 99
Lloyd George, David, 90
Lightbody, Helen, 119
Louis, Prince of Hesse, 44,
 46
Louise, Princess, Duchess
 of Argyll, 24, 26, 30, 32,
 36, 42, 44, 45, 48, 50;
 biographical note, 136
Louise, Princess Royal,
 Duchess of Fife, 56, 59,
 60, 62; biographical note,
 136

Louise, Queen of Denmark,
 55
Lyttelton, Sarah, Lady, 9,
 17–19, 20, 22, 27, 28

Macclesfield, Lady, 54, 58
McDonald, Margaret
 ('Bobo'), 100
Marlborough House, 48, 82,
 83, 119
Margaret, Princess, 7, 9, 11,
 14, 98–100, 103, 104,
 107–10, 112, 114, 115, 119,
 132; biographical note,
 138
Marten, Sir Henry, 112
Marten, Sir Theodore, 50
Mary, Queen, 72, 73, 74, 76,
 78, 80, 82–4, 87, 92, 94,
 96–8, 100, 102, 107, 109,
 118, 119, 121
Mary, Princess Royal,
 Countess of Harewood,
 78, 80, 81, 83, 86, 87, 90,
 91, 94, 98, 108, 114;
 biographical note, 137
Maud, Princess (later
 Queen of Norway),
 58–60, 62, 87;
 biographical note, 137
Mountbatten of Burma,
 Earl, 122, 130

Nicholas II, Tsar, 73

Osborne, 26, 28, 39, 59; as
 naval college, 88, 91, 124

Peebles, Catherine, 124
Philip, Prince, Duke of
 Edinburgh, 9, 10, 109,
 110, 115, 119–21, 124–6,
 130, 132
Phillips, Captain Mark, 132
Ponsonby, Sir Henry, 66

Royal Navy, 42, 65, 66, 78,
 82, 90, 91, 110, 133
Royal Lodge, Windsor, 39,
 99, 104, 107, 109

Sandringham, 48, 56, 58, 59,
 65, 71, 74, 76, 80, 82, 86,
 92, 96, 103, 104, 120
St Peter's Court School, 91
Simpson, Mrs Wallis,
 Duchess of Windsor, 106

Silver Jubilee (of George V),
 104; of Elizabeth II, 133
Stanley, Lady Augusta, 34,
 42, 45, 48
Stockmar, Baron, 17, 30, 31,
 38
Strathmore, Earl and
 Countess of, 93, 96–8, 102
Sullivan, Lady Geraldine,
 69
Swiss Cottage, 26, 32
Synge, Violet, 108

Teck, Princess Mary
 Adelaide, Duchess of,
 72–6
Timbertop (Geelong
 School), 130
Trinity College, Cambridge,
 132

Victoria, Queen, 7, 8, 10, 11,
 13, 14, 16–18, 19–22, 24,
 26, 27, 30, 31, 34, 36, 38,
 40, 42, 43, 44, 48, 50–2, 76,
 78, 86, 96, 109, 118; as
 grandmother, 54–6, 60,
 62, 64, 66, 68, 69, 72; as
 great grandmother, 73,
 74, 80
Victoria, Empress of
 Germany, Princess Royal,
 8, 13, 14, 16, 17, 18, 19–20,
 22, 24, 30, 32, 34, 36,
 38–40, 42, 43, 45, 46, 48,
 50, 58, 73, 76, 96, 118;
 biographical note, 134
Victoria, Princess, 56, 59,
 60; biographical note, 136
Victoria, Princess of Hesse,
 62

Wellington, Duke of, 14, 28,
 46
Westminster Abbey, 84,
 107, 115, 120, 121
White Lodge, 43, 94
Wilhelm II, Emperor of
 Germany, 51, 78
Windsor Castle, 14, 40, 44,
 54, 84, 103, 104, 108, 109,
 110
Windsor, Duke of, *see*
 Edward VIII

York Cottage, 74, 78, 82